BY INVITATION ONLY

By: Margie Harding

This is a work of fiction formed in the mind of the author. Names or events were created for the purpose of this book. Any similarities to names, people or events are totally incidental.

All rights reserved. No part of this publication may be reproduced or transmitted it any form or by any means without written permission of the publisher.

BY INVITATION ONLY

By: Margie Harding

Table Of Contents

Chapter 1	The Contest	5
Chapter 2	The Starlighter Club	22
Chapter 3	Initiation	39
Chapter 4	The Camping Trip	50
Chapter 5	Marlena	68
Chapter 6	Emily	80
Chapter 7	The Promise	87
Chapter 8	The Picture	100
Chapter 9	The Decision	110
Chapter 10	The Dance	117

Chapter 1

The Contest

"Did you get a c-copy of the <u>Viking News</u>?" asked Marlena, brushing her long terra-cotta colored hair from her face.

"Yeah. I got it last period," said Emily, Marlena's best friend, as they worked their way through the maze of students in the hall. "I sure am glad it's lunch time," she continued. "I'm starved!"

"M-Me too, but oh, y-yuck! What's that aw-awful smell?"

"Lunch!" laughed Emily, her green eyes twinkling.

"A-Anyway, as I was saying," Marlena continued, "did you read about the c-contest?"

"That photo thing in the <u>Viking News</u>? I saw it. Didn't read it. You know how I feel about reading!"

"I d-do. About the same way I f-feel about Math! But yes. That photo thing!" laughed Marlena, her voice rising above the din in the lunch room. "D-Don't you think it would be n-neat to win? If you get the w-winning nature p-picture, it goes to the County Photo Contest, too. And there's a c-cash prize to go with it!"

"You really are into this, aren't you?" asked Emily, reaching up to adjust her glasses.

"Y-Yeah," she answered dreamily, falling in line behind Carolyn Paddock, secretary of the Starlighter Club.

"It's a sure bet we'll win that contest," said Judy, the club's vice-president, to Carolyn, who was standing right in front of her. "I'm sure I can talk Dad into letting us use one of his cameras. We'll get some great shots. It's a cinch," she continued, chewing on the ends of her long, dark brown hair.

Marlena wrinkled her face in annoyance. Turning her back to the girls she said in hushed tones, dejectedly, "If the S-Starlighters enter that contest, you kn-know they'll win. It's not fair. They get everything they want. They've all got m-money and they're all popular," she added enviously.

"I don't think they're so great," countered Emily, cracking her knuckles, as she always did when she was annoyed. "I think they're snobs," she said softly.

"Well," said Marlena, shrugging her shoulders, "they are s-snobs, I g-guess. B-But it's easy for you not to care. Your family has lots of m-money, too."

"Lena," said Emily to Marlena's back, carrying her tray to the table, "I wish you wouldn't feel that way."

"Hi guys!" said Emily to Teresa and Terri, already seated at the table.

"Hi, you two. What took you so long? Lunch, whatever it is," said Terri grinning, "is almost over."

Placing her fingertips on her shoulder and batting her eyes dramatically, Emily responded, "We were in line behind the Starlighters. They were talking about how they are going to win the nature contest put on by the school newspaper."

"Oh, that!" laughed Teresa, rolling her eyes.

"Y-You're going to participate, a-aren't you?" asked Marlena. "Emily wasn't real e-excited about it. Th-the winner will be announced at a special dance the school is putting on in two weeks."

"I just haven't thought about it yet," said Emily defensively.

"I'm not sure if I'm entering or not," said Teresa, pulling her long, wavy brown hair behind her shoulders. "You should enter though, Marlena, if you're really interested," she said helpfully.

"I can't," Marlena said matter-of-factly. "Entering was just w-wishful th-thinking on my part. I don't even have a c-camera and I seriously doubt my sister, Cheryl, would let me borrow hers. Even if she d-did, it's a sure b-bet it wouldn't be as good as any Judy's dad has, since he is a p-professional photographer!

"B-Besides I'm different and wouldn't win anyway."

"We're all different," countered Teresa.

"Not like me!"

"No, I don't have Down's, but I do have arthritis."

"And I have diabetes," added Terri.

"And you know I am dyslexic!" added Emily.

"I kn-know that. But I look different."

"It doesn't matter, Marlena. You're smart, pretty and can do anything anyone else can."

"I still stutter, sometimes, too," she added, while stabbing at the food on her plate.

"It doesn't matter. I think you should enter, too," said Terri. "Who knows, you might give the Starlighters a run for their money!"

"W-Well, still. If I had a c-camera I would. But I d-don't. So, I w-won't."

"Well," said Emily thoughtfully, "I do have a nice camera. It may not be as good as Judy's dads, but we could enter the contest as a team if you want."

"You m-mean it?" asked Marlena, hurrying to finish her food. "That's a g-great idea. W-We'll be p-partners," she said, grinning with satisfaction.

"We'll work out the details later," said Emily, picking up her tray. "We've got to get to class or we'll be late."

"I kn-know I have to help M-mom until noon t-tomorrow," said Marlena excitedly and rapidly, causing her stuttering to increase, while leaving the lunchroom. "I a-always do on S-Saturday's. After I'm f-finished, I'll s-see if I can c-come over f-for a while."

"Okay," said Emily as they parted ways. "See you tomorrow."

"Hi, Marlena!" said Mrs. Jackson the next afternoon. "Emily is in her room. You know the way," she added smiling.

"Th-Thanks!" said Marlena walking through the circle living room. She gently traced the edge of the piano as she neared the hallway. I love this house she thought, pausing to look at her surroundings. Standing for another moment she etched in her memory every piece of furniture and decorative accent, vowing one day she would have something as nice as this.

Noting the teal drapes around the French double doors in the dining room with matching carpet and the corner hutch filled with fine china, her heart beat faster. "Someday!" she whispered. "Someday."

"I d-didn't think we'd ever get f-finished c-cleaning the house," complained Marlena, falling across Emily's lavender canopied bed. "Cheryl h-had a special s-soccer p-practice today and d-didn't have to h-help. Rachel and Philip took out their t-toys as fast as I picked them up. Thank g-goodness Zachary is too little to have toys all over the p-place. He still stays in one s-spot!

"B-Boy I wish I were an only child l-like you."

"Well, I hate being an only child," said Emily. "It's boring."

"W-What I'd give for b-boring," laughed Marlena, rolling over. "B-Besides, being an only child, your parents give you everything you want. I mean, look at this room! It's great!"

"I know, but it gets lonely sometimes. I wish Mom would have another baby. I've heard Mom and Dad talk about it. I think Dad wants it, but Mom never sounds too excited with the idea," said Emily, cracking her knuckles.

"I th-think you're crazy. Your l-life is perfect just l-like it is."

Emily took the camera from the night stand beside her bed. "Do you know what you want to get a picture of for this contest?" she asked, changing the subject.

"N-Not really," said Marlena. "B-But we should know it when we see it. N-Nature stuff should be pretty easy. Don't you th-think?"

"Probably," said Emily shrugging her shoulders.

"What's this?" asked Marlena, picking up a pale blue envelope from the bed.

"Oh that?" responded Emily, face askew. "Read it and find out," she added, adjusting her glasses.

Marlena sat up on the bed reading silently. "You got an in-invitation from the S-Starlighters to P-Patti Cooper's induction party?" she gasped.

"Looks like."

"You going?" breathed Marlena.

"No!" she answered emphatically, frowning. "You know I don't like hanging around with them."

"Yeah, but it w-would be so c-cool to go! N-Not everyone gets an invitation like this. Y-You could go; then tell m-me what it's l-like. I w-would give anything to be asked t-to join that c-club," pouted Marlena. "But they'd never let someone like m-me in. Th-They think I have some k-kind of contagious d-disease."

"I don't know what they think," countered Emily. "What I do know is the only one I really like in that group is Carolyn. She's got a great book collection and I think she's the nicest one of them all, too."

"They m-must be thinking about asking you to join," Marlena said in awe. "Think of the p-possibilities. L-Look at it this way. If you get in, m-maybe I have a chance to g-get in, too. You could have some in-influence on them. At l-least go to the party and f-find out what it's l-like. W-What do you have to l-lose?"

"I don't want to go," Emily insisted. "Besides, I thought you'd be mad if I went."

"I'll be m-mad if you don't," quipped Marlena. "L-Look, you've got to g-go," she pleaded. "Y-You may be my only chance of g-getting in."

"I still don't want to go," said Emily softly. "But I guess I could."

"Look, just go to the p-party, report back and then m-maybe I'll get lucky," she said dreamily. "Besides, who kn-knows, you might even have a good t-time."

"All right. All right!" said Emily, laughing at her friend's determination. "I'll go! But now we have to decide where we're going to get these nature pictures for this contest you were excited about yesterday. We only have two weeks, you know."

"I had an idea," said Marlena, beaming with pleasure. "L-Look, next weekend we're s-supposed to go c-camping. If you came, we could t-take pictures there. Besides, you would be someone to talk to. R-Rachel and Philip like playing in the dirt and Cheryl just r-reads and sleeps."

"That's a great idea," agreed Emily, adjusting her glasses again. "You don't think your parents will care if I come?"

"Of c-course not," said Marlena, rolling her eyes. "You're p-practically part of the family!

"Hey, maybe D-Dad would set up the tent f-for us and they can be in the c-camper."

"That would be sweet!" said Emily.

"N-Now, what are you wearing to the party t-tomorrow afternoon?" asked Marlena changing the subject abruptly.

"Who cares?" asked Emily, frowning.

"You better, if you intend to join their c-club."

"I don't want to join their club. Remember? You do," insisted Emily.

"It's all the s-same. You're m-making a good impression for both of us," said Marlena, walking to Emily's closet.

Marlena stood for a moment in silence looking at the clothes. She sighed. "It's not fair," she said, dejectedly. "You have the b-best clothes."

Emily walked across the room to her friend. "You have nice clothes, too," she said softly.

"Sure," replied Marlena sarcastically, immediately regretting her response. "I'm sorry. I didn't m-mean it like that. You know most of mine are handmade." Then reaching for a garment, she said cheerily, "H-Here wear this. It's p-perfect!"

Emily held the white leather skirt and jacket next to her. The silver buttons glistened in the light, the long tassels dangling. "All right," said Emily. "If you think so."

"It blows my mind," Emily continued, "how well you can sew when you don't like Math."

"What's M-math got to do with it?"

"Well, you have to measure and cut and put it all together following a pattern. Isn't that Math?"

"I've never th-thought about that. I don't use a p-pattern."

"Seriously?"

"No. N-Never have. Mom says I have some k-kind of g-gift. I can just picture it and m-make it work."

"You make it work all right. For handmade clothes, they're awesome."

"You're k-kind," murmured Marlena. "It j-just sort of works for me. But h-honestly, I think s-someday, I'd like to get good enough to have my own store with clothes I m-make for other p-people," she added dreamily.

"You'd be good at that," encouraged her friend.

"Well m-maybe. But p-people would have to get past my D-Down's, and I don't know if that's g-going to happen."

"You'll make it happen," said Emily. "I know it. I just know it."

"Thank you," replied Marlena. "Y-You're the b-best friend ever."

The next afternoon Emily checked herself once more in the mirror. The outfit fit her petite frame neatly. She shook her head gently, coaxing her dark hair to loosely lie around her face.

"I wish I hadn't told Marlena I'd go," she said to her reflection staring back at her. "It seems so stupid."

Ten minutes later Emily stood in front of Gail's door. Reluctantly she rang the doorbell.

"Hi," greeted Gail pleasantly. "I'm glad you could come on such short notice. Carolyn was supposed to mail the invitation a week ago, but things got messed up."

"It's okay," said Emily quietly, as she followed her hostess to the entrance of the enormous living room. Inside Emily noted they were moving toward music playing.

"We're in here," said Gail gesturing, as she swished her long, wavy, red hair behind her shoulders. "Hey, everyone," she spoke loudly, attempting to talk over the blaring music. "Look who's here. Emily."

Emily found herself surrounded by the other girls. "Ohhhh. I love your outfit," said Judy.

"Oh yeah, me too" said Patti. "It's beautiful and fits you perfectly," she added dramatically.

Looks like Marlena called that one right, thought Emily, feeling warm and nauseous. She is the fashion diva. I don't believe I came to this. She closed her eyes, trying to find balance.

Without noticing Emily's discomfort, Gail interjected, "Judy has the best record collection. Come on, Emily, let's dance," she said, pulling gently on Emily's arm. "I know Jay or Ricky would love to dance with you. Adam Blake is here too. He's new to our little group. We're growing slowly," she added confidentially. "We want just the right people."

Emily found herself in the center of the room dancing with Ricky Jenkins. His blond hair bounced around his forehead carelessly as his body moved to the fast beat. Emily blushed when Ricky's glassy, blue eyes rested on her for longer than one second.

The music finished, snacks were eaten and again Emily was dancing. Her heart raced with near panic when the pace was changed to slow.

"Hi," said Adam, who was standing nearest her. "Would you like to dance this one with me?" he asked shyly. "I'm not very good but….." He shrugged his wide shoulders.

You can't be any worse than Jay, thought Emily. Now there's someone who really has two left feet. "I guess so," she stammered, blushing again. "I'm not very good either," she added, consoling him.

They moved slowly together. To her surprise, Emily relaxed a bit. "You seem different from the rest of the group," she said softly, immediately wishing her thoughts weren't spoken aloud.

"So do you," he countered, looking directly into her green eyes.

The music stopped, causing their conversation to end abruptly.

"I really need to go," said Emily, turning to Gail. "Thank you for inviting me."

"You have to go already?" questioned Gail, disappointment in her voice. "We're just getting started."

Emily nodded. Two hours is long enough, she thought.

"Girls," called Gail. "Emily is getting ready to leave."

The girls quickly surrounded her, leaving her no escape. "Have you ever thought of joining the Starlighter Club?" asked Gail.

"Uh, no, not really," said Emily, feeling her temperature rise.

"As you probably know, it's only been Gail, Carolyn, and I," continued Judy, "for a long time. And we've just invited Patti," she added, casting an approving look toward their newest member. "We have specific guys we include at functions, although they aren't "really" part of our "all girl" group," she added giggling.

"We thought you would be a nice addition to our group," interjected Carolyn quietly, pleasantly smiling, while twirling her long, straight hair around her fingers, as if it might make it curl.

"Actually, Marlena Richardson is the one you should talk to. She would love to join your club."

"You're kidding? Her? What does she have to offer? Besides, she has Down Syndrome or something weird," said Judy with disdain, placing the ends of her hair into her mouth. "One person we don't need, is Marlena Richardson."

Emily squared her shoulders in determination. "You've got her all wrong. Yes, she has Down's, but she's a wonderful person, and my best friend. And one thing is certain," she continued, her voice steady, "if Marlena can't join, I'm sure not going to."

"Okay, let's not get hasty," said Gail, shooting a disapproving look toward Judy. "Maybe we can work something out," she continued thoughtfully, taking charge. As she pondered, the only thing heard was the consistent flicking of her well-manicured fingernails.

"How about we get together on Tuesday night with Marlena and see what we can do. Maybe she could join the club. We might be able to fine tune the rules of our club, just this once," she added with authority.

"Where did you want to meet?" asked Judy, clearly puzzled by Gail's change of perspective.

"We could meet here, or….wait. Do you think we could go to your house? I almost forgot, Mom and Dad have guests coming Tuesday night. 'Bout 6:30?"

"Sure, no problem," said Judy warily.

Emily looked at the girls around her. What does Marlena see in this club? She asked herself. Why does she want to join a club you can only get into if invited? All they think about is clothes, records and parties. They're fake. "I need to be going now," she said quietly, feeling sick.

"You never said whether you're free Tuesday night," said Gail quickly.

"Probably," said Emily. "You'd really consider letting Marlena join?"

"Sure. Why not?" said Gail. "It could be interesting."

"Well, I'll tell Marlena about the meeting. I'm sure she'll be excited," she added, as she escaped through the front door.

Emily flopped on her bed, all her energy drained. Reaching for the telephone, she pushed the familiar numbers without thought. "Marlena," she began, "you are not going to believe what happened this afternoon."

"T-Tell me," Marlena commanded. "W-What was it l-like? Were there lots of b-boys there? W-What did they w-wear? What was G-Gail's house like?"

"Wait a minute, and I'll tell you," laughed Emily lightly. "It really wasn't all that great. Jay and Ricky were there and Adam Blake. He's new to the group. Remember him from last year?"

"And how c-could I forget?" asked Marlena giggling. "H-He was only the c-cutest boy in the whole school!

"C-Come on, k-keep going," she breathed. "I want every s-single detail!"

"We danced and ate and stuff," Emily responded quietly.

"What s-stuff?"

"Well, they want me to join their club."

"You're k-kidding?" shrieked Marlena. "I kn-knew it. Y-you going to?"

"Well, you already know I don't want to. But I told them you did, so we're supposed to go to a meeting on Tuesday night at Judy's house at 6:30," Emily said, as casually as possible.

"A-And th-then I m-might be able to join? You m-mean I r-really have a ch-chance to join the Starlighters?" gasped Marlena. "I c-can't b-believe it. What will I wear? How w-will I fix my h-hair? It's got to be p-perfect. Everything has g-got to be j-just perfect.

"Oh, Emily, I can't b-believe my d-dream is f-finally coming t-true. Aren't you excited?"

"No, not really. I think the whole idea is just dumb."

"C-Come on. It is not. You're not g-going to ruin this for me. Are you?"

"No, I'm not," Emily conceded slowly. "I know you really want it. But I'm just not into it like you are."

"I-I've got to g-go," Marlena said, shaking with excitement. "I-I can't wait to tell M-mom and Dad. Cheryl will be absolutely g-green with envy.

"Em," she continued, a bit calmer. "Th-Thanks for everything. It'll be p-perfect. You'll see."

Emily sat on her bed thinking of her best friend. She could almost hear Marlena shouting the news to her family.

"What will this do to our friendship?" she asked herself out loud. "Will Marlena change for the Starlighters? Well, if Marlena wants to join, she can. I'm not going to."

Chapter 2

The Starlighter Club

Marlena's hands were sweaty. She looked into the mirror, yet another time. Her crisp, black-denim mini skirt was complimented by a gray shirt featuring white bursting stars and planets. Clean white sneakers and socks, completed the outfit. The wide, black hair-band in her hair complimented her fair complexion, setting off her brown eyes. "E-Emily are you sure this l-looks all right? Or d-do you think this skirt m-makes me look even shorter? You look so much more like a S-Starlighter than I do," she said, exasperated.

"You look fine," her friend assured her. "Would you calm down? You're going to be so uptight, you won't be able to enjoy tonight at all."

"Enjoy?" Marlena snapped. "T-Tonight isn't to enjoy. I-It's my f-future. I just have t-to be p-part of this c-club. If I c-can do this, I can do anything. D-Don't you see?" she asked pleadingly. "I've g-got to show them D-Down S-Syndrome doesn't s-stop p-people."

A twinge of guilt crept over Emily while her heart ached for Marlena. Emily had not yet told her friend she had already decided not to join the club. What would that do to Marlena's chances of joining the Starlighters? *I suppose I should tell her,* she thought. *I can't do that,* she argued with herself, seeing the anxiety in Marlena's face. That would ruin everything. Maybe after tonight, they will see that Marlena does belong in their club, Emily thought hopefully.

Marlena and Emily walked up the sidewalk. The mid-spring evening felt more like mid-summer, as the temperature held steady from the hot day. Trees were filled with new leaves, flowers burst with color everywhere and birds sang their songs of joy in the newness of life. Marlena anticipated that same newness of life with an upcoming change. Emily, on the other hand could scarcely believe she had come this far to something she opposed so strongly. Her stomach felt like knotted chains being pulled tighter with each step.

"W-What a b-beautiful house," whispered Marlena in awe. "I've s-seen it a zillion t-times but I n-never knew J-Judy lived here. L-Look at this p-place!"

Emily knocked on the door. "Door's open," called a familiar voice from inside.

The girls let themselves in. "We're in the den, next to the living room on your right," the voice continued. "Come on in."

"Y-You go f-first," Marlena murmured. "I'm too n-nervous."

The girls followed the sound of the voice. "Hi!" said Judy, coming into the living room. "Sorry I didn't come out sooner. We were finishing our meeting. We've decided to invite Marlena to join the Starlighters, too," she said sweetly. "We were just finalizing your initiation qualifications. Come on in and we'll tell you about them."

Marlena scanned her surroundings. She felt like she was drowning in beauty as she entered the den. The light aqua carpet complimented the darker aqua wallpaper, giving Marlena the sensation of being on the ocean floor. It was cool and refreshing. She noted the elaborately carved desk with all the latest technology devices adorning the uncluttered desktop. The brightly lit, immaculate room ended with a shelf lined wall, filled with books.

Emily sat in the chair nearest the large tropical plant in the corner. Marlena sat next to her, facing her peers, nerves taunt, but for entirely different reasons.

"There are several things you must know about our club," began Gail. "We have some strict rules about who can join, and each person's qualifications are unique. You each have four goals to accomplish. You have ten days to complete your requirements, and you must each promise not to tell the other what she has to do. If you do, you're automatically disqualified. By not telling each other, you prove loyalty and trustworthiness to the club."

"Do you promise not to share with each other or anyone else what you have to do?" asked Judy, picking up where Gail left off.

The two girls looked at each other. Never before had anyone asked them to keep secrets from each other. "I p-promise if Emily does," said Marlena, tingling with excitement.

"Okay," said Emily. The knots in her stomach were tightening. She was cold. Absently Emily rubbed her arms, in an effort, to ward off the chill.

Gail handed Marlena and Emily each a sealed envelope. "Y-You m-mean I'm r-really invited to j-join the S-Starlighters?" Marlena breathed.

"Well, sure. Provided, of course, you meet all the requirements," answered Gail smugly.

"G-Gosh thanks," said Marlena, her heart pounding. "I know I w-will. Th-This is so g-great. I j-just can't b-believe it. Right Emily?"

Emily only nodded. No sound would come from her voice.

"Open your envelopes now, girls. Just remember secrecy is vital," said Judy.

In unison, they opened their envelopes. Gail, with satisfaction, saw the frown flicker across Marlena's face. The cool, refreshing room suddenly felt like a hot steam bath.

Realization came quickly. This is going to be hard, thought Marlena. How am I ever going to do this stuff? She could feel the hand slap her face with contempt. They made this difficult on purpose! I'll bet Emily's isn't like this. She read the list one more time and noted the message on the bottom.

1. Get a lock of hair from Judge Simms personally.
2. Hand deliver flowers to Adam Blake.
3. Join four new clubs.
4. Make sure Emily joins the Starlighters.

    Carolyn knows Judge Simms, so she will know if you really get the lock of hair from him. We all know Adam Blake and will know if you delivered the flowers. It's easy to find out which clubs you joined and it is absolutely essential Emily joins the club for you to be able to. Good luck!

The Starlighters:

Gail, President

Judy, Vice-President

Carolyn, Secretary

Patti, Member

    Marlena fought panic. Good Luck the note said. Well, she'd need it. Marlena folded the piece of paper and carefully placed it back in the envelope. Emily did the same. What does she have to do? Wondered Marlena. What in the world am I going to do? Her heart raced, her palms were sweaty. She noted Gail and Patti talking with Emily. I am going to do this, she thought, with new determination. I am good enough for this club and I aim to prove it!

"I think we should go now," said Emily, cracking her knuckles.

"Uh, o-okay," responded Marlena, standing. She took a deep breath before speaking further. "Th-Thanks for in-inviting me and Emily to j-join your c-club."

"No problem," said Judy smiling sweetly. "Glad to have you. Remember, ten days. That means next Friday night, the night of the dance, to fill all your initiation obligations for joining the club. Good luck and remember, absolute secrecy is a must."

"We remember," said Emily for both of them, walking out the door.

"B-Boy do we remember," said Marlena to Emily when they stepped off the porch and out of earshot of the girls inside the house.

"You know, you don't have to go through with this," said Emily. "I'd rather just forget the whole thing. I don't even think I'm going to do my list. I don't want to join."

Panic filled Marlena's voice. "Y-You have to j-join," she blurted. "You h-have to!"

"No, I don't!" said Emily matter-of-fact. "Just because you want to be part of that group, doesn't mean I have to be."

Neither girl spoke the rest of the walk home, each pondering her own circumstances. The air around them felt heavy and close. They said good-bye quickly as they parted and went to their own homes.

Emily gave an audible sigh of relief as she fell onto her bed, letting her taunt muscles relax. She dug in her pocket for her list from the Starlighters. This is way too easy, she thought, slowly reading the four instructions again:

1. Enter the photo contest.
2. Be on the honor roll.
3. Be at the dance on Friday night.
4. Agree to join.

It made no sense. What could the Starlighters gain with her entering the contest? Perhaps nothing. They didn't know she and Marlena planned to enter together. The honor roll? They were undoubtedly aware she was on that. She had always gotten good grades, even if she did struggle with dyslexia. The dance? Was something special going to happen Friday night?

Emily searched her mind for answers but fell way short and instead fell asleep where she lay.

― ― ―

Four new clubs, Marlena thought flopping into the oversized chair in the living room after returning home. That's the easy part. I can join the Spanish Club, Journal Club, Art club; I hate art, she chided herself wrinkling her nose at the thought, and the Newspaper Club. It'll be tough and Mom will be furious but she'll just have to understand.

Pulling the note from her pocket, Marlena stared at the words with disdain. Adam Blake and Judge Simms are an entirely different matter. Those will be horrible. Marlena leaned back in the comfortable chair and let her mind wander. I have to do this she thought. I have to prove to them I am good enough for their club; and to myself, said the unbidden voice inside her.

Reaching for the phone book, Marlena scanned the pages until she saw what she needed. "M-Mrs. J-Johnson?" she said quickly, "Th-This is M-Marlena R-Richardson. I know it's l-late, and I shouldn't have c-called your h-house, b-but your sh-shop is c-closed. I need a g-giant sized f-favor."

"What do you need, Dear?"

Breathing deep, Marlena plunged ahead. "I n-need to order s-some f-flowers for a f-friend of m-mine. S-Something I c-could p-pick up on my w-way h-home f-from school t-tomorrow." Marlena felt hot and sick to her stomach.

"I'll be glad to help, Marlena," said Mrs. Johnson. "Is there a price range you would like to stay in? Are these flowers for someone who's ill?"

Price? Now that's something she hadn't thought of. Her parents didn't give allowance and she'd already spent most of her report card money. Her mind was reeling.

"Uh, ill, yes. S-Someone is r-real s-sick," she stammered. "A-And c-could we k-keep the c-cost under f-fifteen dollars?" she asked, fighting the urge to slam down the phone.

"I think I can make you a nice arrangement for fifteen dollars," said the woman on the line. "Any particular kinds of flowers you want included, like carnations or daisies? Or do you have something else in mind?"

"N-No. W-Whatever you usually m-make for s-sick p-people will be f-fine," she answered impatiently.

"Very well. It won't be fancy, but nice. I'll take care of it."

"Th-Thank you, M-Mrs. Johnson. I r-really am s-sorry to b-bother you at h-home like this."

"Don't worry about it, Dear. It's not a problem. I just hope your friend feels better."

"Yes, Ma'am."

"I'll see you tomorrow." Marlena put down the phone. Her palms were sweaty, fingers ice cold. *My friend feels fine,* she thought sarcastically. *I'm the one sick with a disease!*

"I've got to talk to Emily," she said aloud, picking up the phone again. Hitting the "favorites" star, she stared at the names. Emily was on top. *If I call her now,* she scolded herself silently, *I'll tell her everything. I can't do that. I just can't.*

"Who were you talking with on the phone?" asked Cheryl, coming into the living room. "It's late. Mom would be mad if she knew."

Spinning, Marlena jammed the note into her pocket.

"You sure are jumpy," Cheryl continued. "Was that your boyfriend?" she teased.

"N-No it w-wasn't," Marlena snapped. "A-And it's n-none of your b-business!"

"Whoa! I was just messing with you. What's the matter, anyway?"

"D-Did you ever w-want to join a c-club?" asked Marlena.

"Sure," said Cheryl, shrugging her shoulders. "It's not a big deal though. I've been in the Spanish Club and the Science Club. Why?"

"Not those k-kinds of c-clubs," said Marlena roughly. "Y-You know. A p-private kind of c-club where only c-certain p-people can join."

31

"Oh those," said Cheryl disgustedly. "No. I've never been in one of those. There was one once. I was asked to join but all the girls were snobs. The only reason they even wanted me in was Larry Peterson, the guy that liked me then, was popular. I told them forget it. Why?" she repeated.

"Well," Marlena started slowly. "I've b-been invited to join the S-Starlighters. Th-They are the c-coolest c-club at s-school."

"Oh pa-lease!" said Cheryl, covering her ocean green eyes with her hand. "Isn't Judy Summers party of that group?"

"Y-Yeah. Why?"

"Her sister, Tracy, talks about them all the time. Even she says they're a snobby little group. And personally, I think Tracy is a little overbearing. I can't imagine what Judy and her friends must be like. You can't be serious about wanting to join them?"

"I a-am. And y-you're just j-jealous."

"Jealous?" laughed Cheryl. "Look, you're only going to get hurt. If they've asked you to join, you can be sure they have an ulterior motive."

"N-No they d-don't," Marlena insisted, feeling defensive, while knowing it was at least partly true. They really do just want Emily, came the unwelcome thought. Dismissing it, she added, "I a-am g-going to j-join the S-Starlighters. Y-You just w-watch!"

"What do you have to do to get in?" asked Cheryl suspiciously.

"I c-can't tell you," barked Marlena. "B-But I am g-going to d-do it."

"Don't say I didn't warn you," said Cheryl, exiting the room. "You're going to be sorry."

"Mom," said Marlena, entering the cluttered kitchen. "D-Do you mind if I c-come home a l-little late t-tomorrow after s-school? I n-need to go to Emily's for a little w-while. W-We need to work on our S-Science p-project that's d-due soon."

Marlena's head ached and her mouth felt stuffed with cotton, while she waited for an answer. She couldn't recall a time she'd ever outright lied to her parents.

"Sure, Honey. But I thought you were working on that last night."

"Y-Yeah, b-but we d-didn't get it all f-finished."

"Just remember, dinner is at 5:30. Don't be late."

Marlena slept fitfully that night. Scenes of Emily, Cheryl and the Starlighters flitted through her mind in tiny, disconnected fragments. Arguments, flowers, and cruel laughter pierced her sleep, leaving her tired and reluctant to face the new day.

"Hi all," said Gail, cheerfully, as she went down the aisle to her desk.

"Marlena, do you feel all right?" she asked, pausing at Marlena's desk. "You look tired. Did you not sleep well?"

Marlena heard the sarcasm in her voice. "I'm fine," she snapped.

"Sorry! I was just asking."

"You know," said Emily after class. "Gail had a point earlier. You do look tired. Didn't you get any sleep last night?"

"Sure, I-I d-did," she replied. "I j-just didn't sleep w-well. I had w-weird d-dreams all n-night. I'll b-be all right."

The morning passed slowly. The clang of the lunch bell jarred Marlena from her stupor. "G-Gosh I'm g-glad it's lunch t-time," she told Emily in the hall. "The d-day is at l-least half o-over."

"Rumor has it you two might be joining the Starlighter Club," said Teresa quietly, as they took their familiar places at the table.

"It's only a possibility," replied Emily, looking at Marlena.

"A g-good possibility," insisted Marlena. "A-All we have to do is their initiation r-requirem-ments. And we're g-going to. R-Right Emily?" She asked pleadingly.

"Time will tell," said Emily, cracking her knuckles.

"Shouldn't you guys be sitting with them, then?" questioned Terri.

"W-We really should go over t-to their table and t-talk with them. Don't you th-think, Emily?" asked Marlena, ignoring the sting of sarcasm in Terri's voice.

"No, this is fine," said Emily, taking her seat.

"Oh, c-come on," chided Marlena. "Let's g-go," she said turning. "I th-think we sh-should."

"I'd rather not," Emily said.

"P-Please?"

Reluctantly, Emily walked with Marlena to the far side of the cafeteria. "Hi, e-everyone," said Marlena with more enthusiasm than she felt. "F-First, Gail, I want to a-apologize for s-snapping at you this m-morning. I didn't sleep g-great last night and I am t-tired to-d-day. And we just w-wanted to come over to say h-hi and thank you again f-for last night. We're b-both excited about joining your c-club."

"Great," said Gail, flicking her fingernails.

Seconds felt like hours for Marlena as the girls searched for something else to say.

"A-Are any of y-you g-going to enter the photo c-contest the p-paper is putting on?" Marlena said, in a rush attempting to continue the conversation. "E-Emily and I are e-entering it to-g-gether. In f-fact, we're going to get p-pictures on a c-camping t-trip this w-weekend."

35

"Yeah, we're going to enter," answered Carolyn in a friendly tone. "Judy's dad has this great camera she's sure he'll let us use."

Marlena's face grew hot. She'd forgotten the conversations she'd over heard in the lunch line only a few days before and her reaction to it.

"I j-just had a w-wild idea," burst Marlena, ignoring the rush of her beating heart. "W-Why don't you g-guys come with us on our c-camping t-trip this w-weekend? We're just g-going out of town to H-Hideaway P-park. I know my p-parents won't mind. It'd be g-great. You c-could get some g-great shots for the contest, too. It'll just be F-Friday night and S-Saturday. We always leave l-late S-Saturday aft-ternoon since there's ch-church on S-Sunday."

Emily stiffened. This weekend was supposed to be for them. How could Marlena do this? She looked at Marlena with pleading eyes.

"C-Come on. W-What do you th-think?" Marlena pressed on carelessly.

"Camping?" asked Gail, her face askew. "Aren't there bugs and snakes and stuff when you go camping?"

"Well, b-bugs maybe, but n-not snakes. At l-least I've n-never seen any when we've c-camped. C-Come on," she pleaded. "You'll l-love it.

"You w-wouldn't even have to w-worry about a t-tent. The one we have is b-big enough for all of us. We even h-have extra s-sleeping bags if n-none of you have any."

"You're going to be on this camping trip, too. Right Emily?" asked Judy.

"Well, I was," she said, with an accusing glare at Marlena.

The girls looked at each other and held a quiet conversation. "Well, all right," said Gail. "Patti says she can't make it, but as President of the Starlighters, the rest of us accept. As long as, you're going to be there, too, Emily. And, of course, we will have to clear it with our parents. But we don't think that will be a problem."

"G-Great!" exclaimed Marlena. "It's s-settled! I'll g-get b-back to you on the exact t-time we l-leave, what you m-might need to b-bring and all that, t-tomorrow. It's gonna b-be a g-great w-weekend," she continued, without looking at Emily.

Marlena and Emily turned to leave. "How could you do that Marlena?" Emily hissed through clenched teeth. "I thought you wanted me to go with you camping. I thought we were supposed to get pictures for the contest. What are your parents going to say? Don't you think you should have asked them first and then asked the Starlighters? I'll bet none of them have even ever gone camping before!"

Marlena listened while her friend voiced all the things running through her mind. "It'll be all r-right," she said, more strongly than she felt. "Mom and D-Dad always told me I c-could invite a friend or t-two anytime I wanted to go c-camping."

"A friend or two is not all the Starlighters, plus me," countered Emily.

"Oh c-come on. It'll j-just be you, G-Gail, C-Carolyn and Judy. N-No b-big deal. You'll s-see. It'll b-be fine," she said, trying to convince herself, as well as, Emily.

Chapter 3

Initiation

Marlena looked at the arrangement of flowers in her possession. Mrs. Johnson's idea of something small and her color combinations sure are different from mine, she thought grimly, looking at the scarlet red carnations and sun yellow pansies splashed between a generous supply of gentle pink bellflowers and pure white impatiens. The arrangement was pretty, she conceded, but feminine and delicate. Not at all masculine. "Ohhhhh," she groaned, louder than she intended.

"Is something wrong?" asked Mrs. Johnson.

"Uh, no. It's b-beautiful. Perfect," she lied. How am I ever going to give this to Adam? she wondered, near panic.

Marlena hurried out the door afraid of more questions she didn't want to answer. She was drained of all energy, as she started down the street, feeling the perspiration drips ripple across her body, while the heat from the pavement made her feet feel like fire through her thin-soled sneakers. The sight of the ice cream parlor intensified the feelings.

Marlena turned off Postet Avenue onto Zella Street and froze in her tracks. Her legs refused to move. They were suddenly filled with lead, much too heavy to carry. Her stomach was doing Olympic sized somersaults, as she came into full view of Adam's house.

With conscious effort, Marlena moved one foot in front of the other until she reached the large front porch. Rockers sat welcoming visitors, as well as, an outdoor porch swing. Marlena swallowed hard, trying to keep from getting sick.

Forcing herself onward, she climbed the four steps to the landing, and stood staring at the doorbell. Prying one hand from the plant, she reached for the tiny circle that would announce her arrival.

Abruptly, the door opened. Marlena jumped. Her face felt fiery red, as she stared blankly into the faces of Adam, Jay and Ricky, obviously getting ready to leave. Her mind went dead. Nearly dropping the flowers, she placed them on the porch with a hard thud and fled. She could feel the eyes bore into her back as she raced down the street, her own spilling over in tears.

Marlena slammed the door to her room and collapsed against it. "W-Why'd they m-make me d-do that?" she sobbed loudly. "W-Why? That w-was h-humiliat-ting!"

"Marlena?" called Cheryl. "Are you all right?"

"I'm f-fine. L-Leave me alone," she snapped, without opening the door.

"Mom wants to know why you came tearing through the house like that. And, you've gotten three phone calls already. One was from a boy named Adam Blake."

"A-Adam called here?" she asked, stunned.

"Yes. Let me in so I don't have to talk through the door."

Marlena opened the door slowly. Cheryl stepped into the room and continued her assault.

"What's this about you joining all these clubs? Mom and Dad will never allow it. You know how they feel about study time and stuff like that."

"I know, I kn-know," said Marlena softly, feeling defeated.

"What are you crying for?" asked Cheryl, suddenly seeming to notice the distress in her sister's face.

"N-Nothing. I'm f-fine," she said, again. Exhausted, she fell across the bed. "T-Tell Mom I'll be out in a little b-bit."

This is awful, she thought, feeling sorry for herself. I can't believe Adam really called here. Emily will just die. She'll never believe it. Marlena shook from a sudden chill. All last year I liked him and he never even knew I existed. Besides that, now I have to deal with Mom and Dad about joining all those clubs, not to mention this camping trip mess I've gotten myself into. And, I still haven't figured out a way to get that lock of hair from Judge Simms yet.

"What else can go wrong?" she spoke aloud, to no one in the room.

"Dinner," came a call from somewhere out her door.

Marlena groaned. This is it, she thought, pulling herself up from the bed.

Picking at her food, Marlena desperately tried to think of a way to casually bring up the subject of camping. Seeing no way to be subtle, she jumped right in. "Mom, D-Dad. You t-told me if I e-ever wanted to invite s-someone to go c-camping with us, you wouldn't m-mind."

"True," agreed her dad, matter-of-factly. "We already told you Emily could come along. Something wrong?"

"W-Well, I'd l-like to invite s-someone e-else," she stated simply, staring at her plate.

"I'm sure we can find room for another friend," offered her mom. "Who is it?"

"W-Well, r-really, it's th-three someone else's," she blurted. Continuing rapidly, afraid that if she stopped she wouldn't get finished; she forged on. "It's the S-Starlighter C-Club, except Patti Cooper. She has p-plans for this weekend. S-See, we have this n-nature photo c-contest at school and c-camping is the p-perfect place for nature ph-photos. So," she breathed deeply, "I invited th-them to c-come along."

"You invited the Starlighters?" Cheryl shouted, dropping her fork. "They're all spoiled brats," she said, with disgust. "Dad, don't let her do this. I couldn't stand it."

"That's enough, Cheryl," her mother spoke sharply.

"You've already invited them?" her father asked, raising his eye brows in a way that annoyed Marlena. "What about their parents? Do they have camping gear? One or two we can handle. But now you're talking about four extra people. You really should've asked us before you asked them."

"I kn-know," responded Marlena in a pleading voice. "This is r-real important to me, Dad. P-Please?" she pressed, casting a wary glance at Cheryl.

"Does this have something to do with you the joining the Starlighter Club?" Cheryl countered. "And I'll just bet you doing the Spanish, Art and Newspaper Clubs do, too. What else are they making you do?"

"What?" her mother barked sharply.

Marlena's face turned red. She felt hot. "N-Nothing I d-don't want to do. So th-there!" she snapped angrily. "Oh, and you f-forgot to m-mention the J-Journal Club," she added.

"D-Dad, p-please. Is it all right if the S-Starlighters come c-camping with us?" she asked, trying to steer the conversation away from the clubs she joined.

"Well," he paused. "I have many reservations about it, but since you already asked them, I don't feel we have much choice. I'll agree; provided," he paused, with jaw set firm, "that their parents have no objection. The next time I expect you to ask us first."

"Th-Thanks Dad!" she said, rushing to give him a hug. "I knew y-you'd understand."

"I'm not sure about understanding," he countered, patting her arm. "It sounds like you're getting in over your head, if this club is making you do stuff just to join."

"I want to know more about this club deal," interjected her mother. "I don't believe you just joined four new clubs. That's way too many. You'll never have time to study or do homework, much less help around here when you're supposed to. Why did you do that?"

"In order f-for me to join the S-Starlighter Club; only the b-best and c-coolest club in the school," she added, "I n-needed to join some c-clubs to show in-involvement—and school sp-spirit," she threw in. "B-Besides, all the meetings, except for Spanish C-Club, are held d-during the day. Spanish C-Club is on Monday after school be-c-cause we get to make the food of the c-country and then e-eat it." She was talking so rapidly, she felt out of breath.

"M-Mom, I'll still be able to h-help around here," she said, softening her tone. "It's j-just one n-night a week. Didn't you e-ever want to do s-something real special in school? J-Joining the Starlighter C-Club is real important t-to me. It'll p-prove I am some-b-body. Somebody sp-special enough to b-belong to the c-club with the most pop-u-lar girls in school. A c-club where you have to b-be invited, to be able to j-join.

"D-Dad, M-Mom," she pleaded. "I c-can handle the extra w-work. It's really, r-really important to m-me to d-do this," she said again, for emphasis. "I'll be c-careful and not let my g-grades slip any. I p-promise."

She waited for an answer. It seemed an eternity. "Well, you can try it out, if your dad doesn't mind," said her mom cautiously. "But no slip ups."

"I-I'll be c-careful. I p-promise," she said, giving her mother a tender squeeze.

Marlena returned to her chair. I am starved, she thought. I can't remember feeling this hungry in a long time. Looking up, she caught Cheryl's glare. She shivered. The hardest part is over, Marlena thought smugly. I think anyway, crept the unbidden words into her mind.

As hard as she tried, sleep alluded Marlena. She tossed and turned until her bed felt like a trampoline. Images of herself silently sneaking into Judge Simms' chambers, snipping off his hair with large, neon, orange scissors, while he slept; then leaving with her prize but handcuffed, walking behind the wrong end of a gun, kept invading the space behind her eyes.

Marlena pulled the covers over her head in a futile attempt to close the curtains on the scenes bouncing around in her mind. "All right s-stop!" she commanded aloud, abruptly sitting up. "Th-There has g-got to b-be a way to d-do this. I will f-figure it out. R-Right now I'm going to sleep!" With determination, she laid back down and shut her eyes tight, refusing to move, willing herself to sleep. Exhaustion won the battle and sleep, although fitful, finally came.

"Let's w-walk to M-Math this way t-today," insisted Marlena, tugging on Emily's sleeve.

"Why? That's the long way," said Emily frowning, adjusting her glasses.

"I know. I-I'd just r-rather," said Marlena, walking away.

"Okay, Okay! Wait for me!"

The girls sped down the hall. Abruptly, Marlena stopped, not giving Kaden Roberts any indication of doing so, causing him to crash into her. Reacting quickly, Emily caught the books Marlena almost dropped. "What's wrong with you?" asked Emily, noticing the boys ahead of them. "You've seen Adam and Jay before."

"N-Nothing. L-Let's go b-back the other way."

"We can't. We don't have time. We'll be late for class."

"I d-don't c-care!" cried Marlena desperately.

"I do, and I'm going on this way," said Emily, continuing forward.

"Ohhhh," groaned Marlena, hiding herself behind Emily.

"Gotten any flowers lately, Adam?" Marlena heard, while quickly darting past the boys. "Gonna get some candy, too?"

46

"Leave it alone," said Adam gruffly, his own embarrassment visible.

"What was all that about?" asked Emily, when she caught up with Marlena seconds later. "Why'd you run past me and the guys like that?"

"N-Nothing. F-Forget it," Marlena choked.

"Sure didn't look like nothing to me," Emily quipped.

"Class," interrupted Mr. Baylor. "Take your seats please."

Alone, in her room later that day, Marlena tried to relax and forget the mid-morning episode. Homework was a trial. Keeping focused was more than she was capable of doing. Exasperated, she walked to the phone. Nervously, she dialed the unfamiliar number.

"I-Is G-Gail in?" she asked, her voice cracking.

"One moment please." The moment seemed like an eternity and Marlena fought the urge to slam down the phone.

"Hello, this is Gail."

"Uh, th-this is Marlena," she stammered. "I was j-just check-ing to see if the S-Starlighters were s-still p-planning to go c-camping; and if you were, what s-supplies you n-needed?"

"Yeah. We're all still going. Everyone has checked with their parents and say it's fine. Judy's folks have an antique tent they said we could use. And Carolyn's mom said she'd send some hot dogs, hamburgers and rolls to help out if your folks would like."

"G-Great!" said Marlena. "I-I'll tell M-Mom. Are y-you sure a-about the t-tent? L-Like I said, ours is b-big enough for us six g-girls."

"No, that's okay. The Starlighters will use Judy's tent and you and Emily can use yours."

"O-Okay, then. T-Try to be h-here by 5:30 tomorrow n-night. We'll l-leave about 5:45."

"No problem. Bye."

Marlena dialed the phone another time. Be there Emily. Be there! "You have reached the Jackson residence. We are not home now….." Marlena slammed down the phone. Overwhelmed by sudden fatigue, she dragged herself back to her room, and collapsed on the bed.

"Marlena," said a voice sharply. "Marlena," it persisted. "Telephone!"

"D-Did I fall asleep?"

"I guess," answered Cheryl, annoyed. "Will you come on? Emily wants you on the phone."

"Oh."

"Hi, E-Em."

"Are you still planning this weekend?"

"S-Sure," said Marlena.

"I don't know if I want to go."

"Y-You've g-got to!" said Marlena, panicking. "It w-won't w-work if you d-don't."

"What does that mean?"

"N-Never m-mind. J-Just c-come like we p-planned. Okay? It'll be g-great. We'll all get to know each other b-better and have a g-great time. The weather's s-supposed to be g-good and our p-pictures will be awesome. R-Remember, we're supposed to d-do that this weekend, t-too. It'll be g-great," she repeated, trying to convince Emily, as well as herself.

"You sure think everything is gonna be great, don't you? Do you realize how many times you said that just now?"

"It d-doesn't m-matter. Are you s-still c-coming?"

"Yeah, I guess so."

"Great! S-See you at school t-tomorrow."

Great, thought Marlena, hanging up the phone. I hope this is 'great.' My future depends on it. I need a great big ton of luck to have all this work out. And I still haven't figured out how to get a lock of hair from Judge Simms. Great! Just Great!

Chapter 4

The Camping Trip

"Here c-comes that s-smell again," said Marlena, weaving her way through the crowd.

"You mean lunch?" laughed Emily.

"Hi, Guys. I see you finally made it," said Teresa, her soft brown curls falling around her face.

"Yeah," said Emily. "We're late. Marlena had to run to her locker."

"Are you sure that's what it was?" asked Terri, her green eyes twinkling mischievously. "I thought maybe it was to visit somebody," she added teasingly.

"W-What are you t-talking about?" asked Marlena, tensing.

"Come on, Terri. Cut it out," said Teresa softly, yet firmly.

Marlena spoke through clenched teeth. "W-Will somebody p-please tell me what's g-going on?"

"Oh, Terri's just teasing you about the latest rumor," said Teresa quietly. "It's going around that you like Adam."

Marlena's face grew hot. "The flowers," she said under her breath.

"What?" asked Terri.

"She said the flowers," answered Emily, adjusting her glasses absently.

"Why'd you take those to him anyway?" pressed Terri.

"It's part of initiation requirements for the Starlighters," stated Emily, flatly, while looking at her friend sadly.

"I'm g-getting l-lunch," said Marlena, walking away.

"Forget it, Marlena," said Emily, catching up with her.

"F-Forget what?" she snapped. "The r-rumor?"

"Well, yeah. That, too. Forget this whole Starlighter business. You don't have to join that club."

"Oh, y-yes I do," she blurted, eyes wide. "I have to p-prove to myself and every-b-body else I know, that I am s-somebody! And as s-soon as I'm f-finished eating this st-stuff that's supposed to be l-lunch, I'm g-going over to their t-table to make sure everything is set for t-tonight."

A gray cloud seemed to loom over the lunch table. Marlena stared at her plate and Emily just picked at her food. Terri could think of no way to ease the tension. Teresa, the quietest of the group, was even more reserved than usual. The clinking of forks and knives and endless chatter reverberated all around them. Instead of friendly chatter, there was only heavy silence.

No one spoke, but watched as Marlena left the table. "H-Hi ev-everyone," she said, pasting her best smile on her face, so the Starlighters wouldn't detect her nervousness. "J-J-ust checking to m-make sure we're all set for t-tonight."

"Where's Emily?" asked Gail.

"She's f-finishing l-lunch. She'll be h-here in a little b-bit."

"I think we're all ready for tonight," continued Gail, flicking her fingernails in annoyance. "Judy has the tent we'll be sleeping in and we all have sleeping bags and flashlights. Oh, and I meant to ask," she said, stroking her long, wavy, red hair. "We will be able to use our curling irons for our hair in the morning. Right?"

"Uh, well, th-there's electric in the l-ladies room, I guess. I d-don't usually worry t-too much about my hair when we c-camp."

"Well, you don't expect me to look dippy all weekend, do you?" asked Gail incredulously. "I have to do my hair."

"O-Okay. B-Bring 'em. L-Like I said you can use the elec-t-tric in the ladies r-room."

"Here comes Emily," said Judy.

"Hi," said Emily quietly.

"You okay?" asked Carolyn, softly.

"I'm fine," she lied. "And there's the bell," she added, relief in her voice.

"R-Remember. M-My house, 5:30. See you t-tonight. And don't f-forget your c-cameras," Marlena said, above the increasing roar of voices and chairs being pushed under the tables.

"Okay," she heard, not sure which one had answered.

"I hope all this turns out like you plan," commented Emily, as they walked toward class.

"I-It'll be f-fine," said Marlena, her stomach in knots. This seems harder than it should. Why do I feel like this? She wondered. I'm scared to death. They're just girls, like me. No, not like me, she thought angrily. They're rich, and beautiful; and I'm poor, not even pretty and I have Down's. Who am I kidding? I have a right to be scared to death!

"Marlena, have you heard anything I've just said?"

"What?"

"Where is your mind. I asked you if it'd be all right if I came over around four o'clock. Mom and dad are going out tonight since I won't be there."

"S-Sure! Four o'clock is f-fine. You don't have to ask that!"

By 5:30, the Richardson household was a fury of activity with last minute details being recalled for the trip. "Okay," said Mr. Richardson, as they loaded the last of the gear in the large van. "Do we have everybody, and everything?"

"I think so," someone responded.

"Well then, here we go!"

One hour later, the Starlighters, Richardson's and Emily set about the task of setting up tents. "Judy, G-Gail, you g-guys want some help with that?" offered Marlena. "D-Dad's good with t-tents."

"It's just that this one is new," lamented Judy. "And I haven't ever put it together. Dad went and bought it just for this trip."

"That f-figures," muttered Marlena under her breath.

"What?"

"Oh, n-never m-mind," she said, recovering. "I'm sure D-Dad will g-give you a h-hand, if you w-want it."

"You d-did bring your S-Star Wars n-night shirt you said I c-could wear this weekend; right Em?" questioned Marlena, moments later in the tent she and Emily shared.

"Oh, I forgot it," said Emily, sighing. "I'm sorry. It totally slipped my mind."

"Thanks a l-lot," spurted Marlena, crossly. "You p-promised you'd b-bring it."

"I was going too. Honest. I just forgot."

"No, you d-didn't," Marlena accused. "You w-wanted to embarrass me in f-front of the Starlighters. N-Now what am I g-going to wear?"

"Come on. That's not fair. You know I wouldn't do that. Did you really not bring anything else to wear?"

"What in the world?" asked Carolyn.

"I think Marlena and Emily are having an argument," said Judy gleefully. "Maybe if they stop being friends, Emily will join our club."

"Judy!" scolded Carolyn. "They've been friends a long time."

"Just l-leave me alone for a w-while," they heard Marlena say. "J-Just leave me b-be."

"I am sorry," said Emily. "I'll let you wear something else I brought."

"I w-wanted your Star Wars shirt," stated Marlena flatly. "And y-you f-forgot it. Or so you s-say, anyway!"

"Dinner!" called Mrs. Richardson.

"Carolyn, thank your mom for the extra hot dogs and hamburgers. That was real nice," she added as the girls took their seats.

"Okay," said Carolyn.

"That's some tent you have there, Judy," remarked Mr. Richardson.

"Thanks," said Judy. "Dad bought it just for this trip."

"I heard that. That was very nice of him," Mr. Richardson replied.

Marlena rolled her eyes and groaned. Cheryl nudged her. "C-Cut it out," hissed Marlena.

"You!" said Cheryl sharply.

"Okay, girls. Stop. Cheryl, how about you helping with clean up and let Marlena and her guests take a walk around the park."

"Mom!"

"Cheryl!"

"Thanks, Mrs. Richardson. You sure?" asked Emily. "I don't mind helping."

"No. Go on. We'll handle it. You can help another time."

"Th-Thanks Mom," said Marlena. "Let's t-take a walk then," she continued, pleased with the chance to escape dish drudgery.

"That sure was a quick walk," noted Cheryl, only fifteen minutes later. "You come back to help?"

"N-No," barked Marlena, disgustedly. "We're going to read. No one s-seems to have anything to t-talk about," she said, glaring at Emily. "B-Besides, we need to t-turn in early anyway, if we're g-going to get p-pictures early t-tomorrow morning. It's t-too dark for p-pictures now."

"Well, the weather is supposed to be good for it tomorrow," Mr. Richardson, offered. "I'm getting ready to start the campfire. Don't you girls want to roast marshmallows and have S'mores?"

"No thanks! Burnt marshmallows are awful!" replied Judy.

"I don't like marshmallows at all," said Carolyn. "Besides, the mosquitoes are biting."

"I like 'em all right, but if no one else wants them, count me out too. We'll just talk in our tent for a while. Thanks, though," agreed Gail.

"Marlena? Emily? You two love roasting marshmallows."

"Not anymore," said Marlena. "Besides, that's kid's stuff. We'll just talk, too."

"M-Mind if Emily and I come in y-your tent with you g-guys for a while?" she continued.

"Sure," answered Gail, lightly. "Help yourselves."

"I think I'd rather just go to our tent and read," said Emily. "You can go if you want to," she said, unzipping the tent flap, stressing her displeasure.

Marlena clenched her teeth tightly. "I th-think I'll d-do just that," she responded tartly.

"So, how are you doing on your initiation requirements?" asked Gail smugly. "Any problems?"

"S-Some, but I'll m-manage," Marlena acknowledged, feeling the beads of sweat on her brow.

"Ummm," snickered Judy, nodding. "Good."

After a short silence that felt like an eternity, Marlena remarked, with greater confidence than she felt, "I think I'll just g-go over to my t-tent and read with E-Emily."

"If you're sure," offered Carolyn, twirling her hair around her finger. "You're welcome to stay."

"N-No, I'm going to go r-read," Marlena stated, already unzipping the screen door.

Barely suppressed laughter followed Marlena to her tent. "Didn't expect you here so soon," snapped Emily.

"R-Read and leave m-me alone," retorted Marlena. "You c-could have b-been there, t-too. You're just t-trying to m-make this h-hard for me."

Emily looked at her friend. Guilt swept over her for non-support, compounded with pity over the change in Marlena, and a newfound anger at what the Starlighters have done to their friendship.

"Marlena," began Emily, softly.

"L-Like I s-said," Marlena cut in. "R-Read and l-leave me a-alone."

"Fine!" huffed Emily.

Marlena pulled the sleeping bag further over her head. The early morning sounds were already invading the tent space. *I'm not ready to get up yet*, she thought angrily. Turbulent scenes from the previous evening collided with the cheer of life coming from the birds singing all around her. "Ohhh," she groaned aloud.

Laying there, she pondered the upcoming day and the possibilities. *Why is this so important to me?* She berated herself. *None of the Starlighters even want me in their stupid club. They just want Emily. I'll show them! I'll finish that impossible test and they'll have to let me in.*

"You awake, E-Emily?"

"Sorta," she said, wearily.

"Well, w-wake up all the w-way," Marlena gushed with as much enthusiasm as she could muster. "I think M-Mom's up starting b-breakfast. I hope Cheryl h-helps her so I d-don't have to."

"You're terrible," Emily giggled.

"You j-just think that b-because you're an only child."

"Don't remind me," she said softly. "You don't know how lucky you are."

"Y-Yeah, right."

"Oh, y-yuck! It's c-cold out here!" gasped Marlena, crawling out of her sleeping bag. "Oh n-no! L-Look outside," she wailed. "It's c-cloudy and it looks l-like it c-could rain any t-time!"

"I thought it was supposed to be hot and sunny."

"W-Well, someone f-forgot to t-tell the sky!" Marlena said, dejectedly. "H-How in the w-world are we going to get p-pictures with the weather l-like this?"

"Sounds like the Starlighters are up," sighed Emily.

"L-Let's go see," Marlena urged, heading for the tent.

"G-Gail, Carolyn, J-Judy. You g-guys up?"

"Sorta," Judy yawned.

"I'm headed for the ladies room" announced Gail. "No one's going to see my hair like this."

"G-Gail, no one c-cares. We're c-camping. B-Besides, the weather is awful. So m-much for sunny! I'm even g-going to go f-find a jacket. It's c-cool out here this m-morning. Besides all that, M-Mom has breakfast going."

"I'll be back," Gail insisted. "I'm going to do my hair."

Emily walked up to the picnic table loaded with paper plates, cups and plastic ware, along with containers of juice and tins of homemade cinnamon rolls. The smell of coffee came from the pot on the campfire, already smoldering with hot coals. Bacon was simmering on foil on the outside grill, and wrapped, roasted potatoes were warming in the coals. "Can I help you with anything, Mrs. Richardson?"

"No, I'm fine, Em. Go enjoy yourself."

"Yeah, right," she murmured under her breath.

"Excuse me?"

"Nothing."

"Well, Okay. Would you tell Marlena I need her a minute, please?"

"Sure."

"Marlena," she called, while heading into the tent. "Your mom wants you a minute. I'm headed on down to the bathhouse. I'll be right back."

"Okay. I'll c-catch up. The S-Starlighters already left. G-Gail had to do her h-hair," she mocked, rolling her eyes.

"I know. I heard," she said flatly. "See you in a few."

"Emily," Judy beamed. "Where's Marlena?" she continued looking around her new friend.

"Her mom wanted her. She'll be here in a minute."

"Good. It gives us a chance to talk alone for a few. Tell us you'll join our club. We really think you'd fit right in," she stressed.

"I'm really not interested. Marlena wants to join. Let her. She's great. She's not wealthy, but she's a good person."

"We don't want Marlena. We want you," Gail insisted.

"Shh. Marlena's coming. We'll talk later," commanded Judy who was nearby.

"Breakfast!" called Mrs. Richardson, to the girls, hoping to be heard. "Come and get it!"

"Thanks for breakfast, Mrs. Richardson," complimented Emily after everyone was finished eating. "It was very good."

"Yeah, thanks!" chimed in the Starlighters in near unison, suddenly remembering their manners.

"Why don't you girls go try to get some pictures before the weather gets any worse," suggested Mr. Richardson, noting his damp chair from an early morning rain shower. "Cheryl will help with clean up."

"Dad," whined Cheryl. "Again?"

"Can we go, too?" asked Willow.

"Please?" begged Philip.

"Fine with me," encouraged Emily.

"M-Mom, I d-don't want the l-little ones t-to c-come. This is important. W-We don't n-need them to t-tag along."

"Sorry guys. You have to stay here. Maybe later we'll go for a walk. Okay?" she coaxed soothingly.

"E-Everybody r-ready?" questioned Marlena, assuming the lead. "This should b-be g-great!"

"I hope it doesn't rain before we get back," commented Judy, looking at the huge gray clouds looming over them. "My shirt would be ruined."

"We n-never wear g-good clothes c-camping," Marlena remarked. "You j-just never know when you're g-going to get d-dirty."

"I don't have any old clothes," countered Judy, causing Carolyn and Gail to giggle.

Marlena reddened. "Well, I do," she said sheepishly.

"Look," commanded Emily quietly staring into the distance.

"Where? At what?" asked Gail.

"Over there, past that big oak tree," she whispered.

"What oak tree?" questioned Carolyn.

"Right there!" Emily gestured, exasperated. "By that oak tree! Don't you see the baby fawn with her momma?"

"Oh, wow!" breathed Gail, finally seeing the wildlife.

Smack! "Darn mosquitoes! They won't leave me alone," whimpered Judy, causing her to nearly drop the camera, as she hurried to set it up on the tripod she brought along.

Marlena raised the camera Emily loaned her, snapping pictures quickly. Abruptly the deer leapt away.

"I didn't get any pictures," whined Judy. "The deer left too fast."

"You'd probably do better if you didn't use the tripod," offered Emily. "Animals are very quick and run away if people come around."

"I know that," answered Judy, sarcastically.

"Just trying to help," uttered Emily.

"I know. I'm sorry I snapped at you."

Slowly the girls moved on, taking occasional pictures of flowering bushes and bursts of flowers in the area around them. The smell of wet ashes and smoke from nearby campfires, was heavy in the air. The threatening clouds and dampness dulled their spirits as much as it had the day itself.

"I n-need to use the c-comfort station," announced Marlena, as the building came in sight. "Anyone e-else?"

"Nope," each girl responded in turn.

"We can wait here until you come back," suggested Gail glibly.

"O-Okay. "I'll only b-be a m-minute," she conceded, breaking into a run.

"Listen. This gives us a minute to talk again before Marlena gets back," gushed Gail. "As President of the Starlighters, I can say for all of us, we really want you to join our club, Emily. I know Marlena is your friend and all, but you're the one we really want. Besides, we already told you and her, if she does the initiation requirements she can join too."

"That's right," encouraged Judy. "And just think of the boys you'd attract. We all know the guys like us because of our club. We're a special group."

"And," Gail cut in, "Everybody that's somebody wants to join our club. But since we're very selective for just the right person, we've selected you."

"Thanks, but I'm not really interested in all the boys you talk about or in joining. I just haven't decided yet," she objected. "Marlena is a nice person and my best friend. I have to admit though, I don't understand why it's so important to belong to a club where the only way in is to be invited."

"Why are you being so difficult?" Gail snapped.

"Why are you being so nasty? I can't help how I feel about it," protested Emily, watching her friend return. "I can't," she repeated, suddenly spinning around, and starting to run.

"E-Emily. W-Where are you g-going?" called Marlena, rejoining the group.

"Let her go," said Gail.

"Just leave me…. Oh no!" Emily spluttered.

"E-Emily? You okay? E-Emily?"

"I just fell," she remarked, reddening as the girls encircled her. "Look at me. I'm a mess! Look at all this mud."

"I'm going back to the tent to change," she added dejectedly. "You guys can keep going. I'm done."

"It's a g-good thing you're w-wearing old clothes," quipped Marlena, casting a smirk at Judy.

"I'm not going on," countered Carolyn. "We should all go back. It's starting to drizzle again. We've probably got all the pictures we can for now, anyway. Come on. I'll help you up," she said, offering her hand.

"I can do it," croaked Emily. "Thanks anyway," she added, looking away.

"Why d-did you do th-that?" snapped Marlena, after they reached their tent.

"Why did I do what; fall in the mud?" she barked in return.

"N-No! Why d-did you t-treat C-Carolyn so mean when she t-tried to help you up?"

"You really don't get it, do you?"

"G-Get what?"

"They are using you to get me to join their stupid club. I'm not joining. I can't believe how this has changed you. I'm not like them and neither are you. At least you didn't used to be!"

"I'm beg-ginning to think I am m-more like them than I am y-you," retorted Marlena.

"I'm glad your folks decided to end this trip early. I'd rather be at my own house than share this tent with you anyway!"

"F-Fine!" shouted Marlena. "I'm g-glad we're going home, too! And here's your s-stupid c-camera!" she added, tossing it on the sleeping bag. "I d-don't want to be p-partners with you anymore. I'll f-find another p-partner or do it myself!"

"Well, fine! Don't be my partner. I don't care!" fumed Emily, pushing at her glasses. "Go be partners with the Starlighters!"

"F-Fine!" Marlena said, defiantly. "I will!"

Chapter 5
Marlena

Marlena pulled the covers over her head, trying to drown the sound of the alarm. Bright sunshine streamed through the windows, joyously announcing morning was here.

Reluctantly, Marlena thought about her upcoming day. After this past weekend, she knew it was going to be tough. Emily and she hadn't been this angry at each other since second grade. Oddly enough, she remembered, thinking out loud, "that was over something I had wanted, too; her new doll I wanted to take home with me for the weekend. She wouldn't let me. I was so mad at her."

Marlena chuckled to herself. That was so silly. I played with it every time I went over there. She sighed. Now we're fighting again.

But this time it's important, she reassured herself. I'd be somebody if I could just join this club. I still don't know why she won't. If she was my friend at all, she'd understand *how* important!

Well, she just doesn't matter anymore. I can still join if I pass the initiation requirements. Gingerly, Marlena pushed back the covers, squinting through the sunshine. Reaching up, she took the note from her night stand. She read it again.

1. Get a lock of hair from Judge Simms personally. I still don't have a clue how that's going to happen, she frowned.

2. Hand deliver flowers to Adam Blake. Done! I'm glad, too. Adam has his stupid flowers. That was positively humiliating.

3. Join four new clubs. Did that too, even though Mom and Dad didn't like it.

4. Make sure Emily joins the Starlighters.

Marlena froze. I forgot she has to join, too, she grunted. Well. I've gotten at least two done, she consoled herself. But now I have no camera for the contest and I still need to figure out how to get Emily to join the Starlighters. Guess I could go over and try to talk some sense into her. She's got to do this for me. Besides what are best friends for? she asked herself, angrily. She gets everything she ever wants. It's not fair. It's my turn!

Climbing out of bed, Marlena donned her favorite outfit: perfectly fitting blue jeans with holes in the knees partnered with a three-quarter sleeved, V-necked, sky blue button down the front top, and prepared for the challenge of the day.

"Breakfast!" she heard from downstairs. "Marlena!"

"C-Coming,"

"You still upset over that argument you had with Emily?" questioned Cheryl, noting Marlena was only picking at her food.

"S-Sort of. W-What of it?"

"Well, if it's about the Starlighters, I still think you're crazy for wanting to join. Look how they acted on the camping trip. They worried about their hair and wore their best clothes. Like, who cares? No one wears good clothes camping. Poor Emily. It's a shame one of the Starlighters didn't fall in the mud instead of her. It would have served them right!" smirked Cheryl, smiling with pleasure at the scene she formed in her mind.

"J-Just s-stop!" snapped Marlena.

"Uuuhhhh, touchy, touchy," needled Cheryl, acting wounded.

"You gonna make up with Emily at school today?"

"M-Maybe. I might n-not even see her."

"You have to see her! You have classes with her."

"W-Well, just t-two. Geography and M-Math. Well, th-three," she corrected herself, "if you include H-Health t-twice a week. B-But I still m-might not g-get a chance to t-talk to her. I was th-thinking, though, I m-might go over to her house after school for a m-minute. I d-do need to t-talk to her; talk some s-sense into her, e-even."

"She doesn't want to join this stupid club, does she?

"J-Just s-stay out of it, Cheryl. Okay? I c-can h-handle E-Emily. She is my b-best f-friend. R-Remember?"

"Sure I do," agreed Cheryl. "But are you her best friend?" she argued.

"G-Get a life," Marlena barked. "I'm l-leaving. You c-can find someone else to walk to school w-with. I'm out of h-here."

"Besides, if you leave now, you'll miss Emily, won't you?" goaded Cheryl.

"S-So what?" Marlena growled. "It'll g-give me t-time to think about how to ch-change Em's m-mind about this whole th-thing."

"Marlena you're awful. Let her alone about it. Just because you want to join, doesn't mean she has to."

"Yes," Marlena stopped abruptly.

"Yes, what?" Cheryl demanded. "Is that part of their initiation stuff? The only way you can join is if Emily does, isn't it?" she asked realizing the answer, as she asked the question.

"N-None of your b-business," Marlena retorted, quickly stalking out the door before any further questions could be asked.

Morning classes dragged by. Fifty minutes felt more like five hours. Emily looked away every time Marlena glanced her direction, leaving her empty and rejected. The Starlighters talked only with each other, strengthening the feeling. I might as well be an outcast, she thought, getting more irritated. This is ridiculous. I am not the bad guy here!

The lunch bell rang. "Marlena, can I see you for a minute before you leave class?" her Geography teacher said.

"S-Sure Mr. Bakworth. Anything wrong?"

"I could ask you the same thing. You were here in body today, but your mind was certainly elsewhere."

"I'm s-sorry. I d-didn't m-mean to be."

"It's not like you. Can I help with whatever is bothering you?"

"N-No thanks. It's j-just s-something I have to w-work out."

"See that you do, then."

"Y-Yes, Sir."

"Hi" said Terri cheerfully. "Why are you so late today?"

"Mr. Bakworth wanted me for a s-second. Th-that's all."

"Well, Emily is already in the lunch line. She'll be back in a minute."

"That's f-fine," said Marlena, dismissing the information.

"You okay?"

"Y-Yup. W-Wonderful!" she quipped.

"Marlena." Turning she tried to narrow down where the sound of her name came from, above the clatter of silverware and mixed up voices in the lunch room.

"MarrrLeeeNaaaa."

Scanning the area, she noted Gail waving her arms broadly.

"Come here," Gail encouraged, motioning with her hand.

"Looks like the famed Starlighters want you," goaded Terri.

"M-Maybe they d-do!" she snapped.

"Sor-ry!" giggled Terri.

"H-Hi guys!" Marlena breathed cautiously.

"Hi, yourself! Pull up a chair."

For the first time all day, her spirits rose. "Thanks," she bubbled, her heart beating faster.

"I r-really am s-sorry for the way this weekend t-turned out. It was awful!"

"Hey, it wasn't your fault. You don't control the weather."

"I know, b-but s-still, I wish it had b-been b-better. We hardly t-took any p-pictures and that was half the r-reason for g-going."

"We were just talking about that," agreed Judy. "How about meeting us at Muddy Creek Park after school today so we can get some more?"

"I d-don't have a c-camera anymore," lamented Marlena, gazing at her hands in her lap.

"I've got one you can use," offered Carolyn helpfully. "Oh, but that means we can't do it this afternoon, because it's at home. I could bring it tomorrow.

"Do you think we could wait until tomorrow afternoon to go to the park?" she questioned the other club members.

"T-Tomorrow would really s-suit me b-better," encouraged Marlena. "I've g-got p-plans this afternoon."

"It's settled then. Tomorrow right after school we'll go to the park, and you can use Carolyn's camera," confirmed Gail, assuming her role as President of the Starlighters.

"G-Great!" bubbled Marlena, her spirit fully buoyed.

"W-What about E-Emily?" inquired Marlena, suddenly remembering her friend.

"What about her?"

"Is she c-coming t-too?"

"Oh, I don't know. Haven't had a chance to ask her yet. If not, I'm sure she'll come around later. She has reason, to, doesn't she?" remarked Gail smugly. "She is your best friend. Right?"

"R-Right," agreed Marlena, her brightened mood deflated.

"You'd better hurry if you plan on eating," mentioned Carolyn. "They're about to close the serving door."

"Oh, y-yeah. I g-guess I'd b-better," Marlena nodded, as she rose to leave.

"Oh, I'm s-sorry," she sputtered, before she realized who she'd collided into. "I d-didn't m-mean to bump into y-you."

"It's okay. It was really my fault," the boy replied.

"A-Adam," quaked Marlena, reddening. "H-Hi," she murmured.

"Hi," he responded, shifting his weight to his other foot nervously. "Can I talk to you a second?"

"S-Sure," she answered quickly. "B-But you'll have to t-talk while I g-get l-lunch, or I'm n-not going to g-get any."

"Okay," he chuckled, following her to the lunch line, ignoring the snickering behind them.

"W-What's up?" asked Marlena coolly.

"Well," hesitated Adam. "I was wondering if you'd let me buy you a soda after school at the ice cream parlor?"

"T-Today?" she bleated, her eyes wide.

"Well, yeah."

"I c-can't. N-Not t-today," she mumbled.

"Another time, maybe," he suggested shyly. Turning abruptly, Adam left, leaving Marlena speechless and completely confused. Recovering, she took her lunch tray and sat at the table where Terri and Emily were finishing their lunch.

"A-Adam just offered t-to b-buy me a s-soda at the ice c-cream p-parlor t-today," she exclaimed with wonder.

"You're kidding?" said Terri. "Isn't he a Straighter Groupie?"

"Well….. W-Wait a m-minute. What g-gives? H-He just d-did that b-because I'm g-going to be joining the S-Starlighters," she uttered exasperated, with the realization.

"Isn't that what you wanted?" pointed out Emily, softly.

"W-Well yeah, b-but. Oh, never m-mind. You just d-don't understand, d-do you?"

"I'm not sure you do," she taunted, leaving the table. Marlena stared after her friend.

Glad the school day was over, Marlena welcomed the momentary refuge of her home and finally her room, as she closed the door behind her quietly, hoping no one had seen her enter the house. "Thank g-goodness," she breathed speaking aloud, leaning against the door.

I have got to get a hold of Judge Simms. What on earth am I going to say to him? Oh, by the way, I need a lock of your hair so I can join the Starlighters? No! That would never do, she chided herself. Calm down and think, she ordered.

Just call and see if you can see him, she commanded. Worry about the rest later.

Okay, she thought. I've got this. The phone book! I need the phone book and I left it downstairs, she moaned.

"Marlena, what are you doing?" Cheryl asked, sounding annoyed.

Startled, Marlena jumped. "N-None of your b-business. Where's the t-telephone b-book?"

"What for?"

"I t-told you, it's n-none of your b-business."

"Fine! Find it yourself!"

"I n-need the phone b-book for a homework assignment," she groused.

"Homework?"

"Well, yeah," she answered. After all, she reasoned it was work she had to do from home.

"I think it's in the kitchen. You okay?"

"S-Sure. W-Why wouldn't I b-be?"

"I don't know. You're just acting weirder than usual."

"S-Sorry," she peeped, spotting the book. "Thanks!" she added, darting away to the seclusion of her room.

Scanning the pages, she finally stopped. County Government. Circuit Court. Judges' Chambers. Judge

Martin Simms would be there. Now that I have the number, all I have to do is call, without Cheryl hearing. Why can't I have my own phone like Emily? She whined to herself. I'd settle for a wireless phone for the whole house. I can't believe we even still have a land line! No one else in the county does, probably not even the state!

Quietly, she left her room again. Seeing no one in the living room, she picked up the phone. "H-Hello. This is M-Marlena R-Richardson. I'd l-like to t-talk with Judge S-Simms, p-please," she said, her heart racing.

"H-He isn't? I n-need what? An a-appointment? C-Can't I just t-talk with h-him on the phone? It's f-for a school p-project. No. I d-don't want h-him to c-call me b-back. B-But I really n-need to t-talk to h-him."

"Okay, I'll b-be there t-tomorrow at f-four. Thanks."

"Marlena. You okay?"

"S-Sure, M-Mom. Why w-wouldn't I b-be?"

"Well, you were sitting there with your eyes closed and your hands clenched shut. You look like you're scared to death."

"N-No, I'm f-fine," she lied, jamming her fist with the phone number in her pocket. "B-But I d-do need to g-get some air. In f-fact, is it okay if I r-ride over to E-Emily's h-house? I n-need to talk to her."

"Sure, for a little while. Just don't be long. Be home in time for dinner."

Malena retrieved her bike from the garage. What a day, she thought, exhausted and shivering, even though it wasn't cold. Now all I have to do is try to reason with Emily.

Chapter Six

Emily

"Mom, have you got a minute? I really need to talk with you."

"Sure, Honey. What's wrong?"

"Well, it's kind of stupid, but Marlena and I aren't getting along at all. And that's the understatement of the year!"

"You two have had arguments before."

"Yeah, but this is different. Marlena's changing. She wants to be part of the Starlighter Club. And I don't want to."

"So let her. It doesn't mean you have to."

"But it does, Mom. My joining is the only way Marlena can join."

"I don't understand."

"It's complicated."

"So explain it to me."

I know someone's here, Marlena thought after knocking on the storm door. The door's open. Without further thought, Marlena entered the Jackson home as she'd done many times before.

Following the sound of voices, Marlena passed the piano near the hallway. "Hello," she called, continuing down the hall.

"So anyway, now Marlena's mad at me because I don't want to join that stupid club and she does."

Marlena froze as several emotions overtook her. Anger, hurt, and then betrayal.

"Mom, why do I have to be an only child? If you'd had more kids I wouldn't even need Marlena," she blurted, angrily. "It's all your fault. Marlena's lucky to have all those brothers and sisters. She never has to be alone. I'd be happy if I had just one sibling!"

"No, it isn't my fault. It isn't anyone's fault," Mrs. Jackson reflected quietly, suddenly emotional.

Marlena tried to move. Her feet seemed glued to the carpet. She'd been taught to never eavesdrop on people's private conversations, but despite her best efforts, she was frozen from fear of discovery and an unexplained curiosity as to why the Jackson's only had one child.

Still, she thought, Emily's the lucky one. I hate having such a large family. Someone is always butting in when you want private time. Mom and Dad never have the money for the neat stuff like Emily has, like your own phone or a piano. What I'd give for my own phone, piano lessons or new clothes instead of hand me downs all the time, or even me making them. Marlena scoffed at the thought. Me the lucky one? Yeah, right! Emily doesn't know how good she has it!

Voices interrupted Marlena's thoughts. "What are you talking about?" she heard Emily ask.

"A long time ago, not long after your Dad and I were married, I became pregnant. Your dad and I were very excited. My pregnancy was normal, but when I delivered, there were problems. We lost the baby after two days. Her little heart failed," Mrs. Jackson said sadly.

"Anyway," she continued, chocking back a sob, "I knew I could never endure that pain again, so your dad and I decided to adopt you, rather than risk me becoming pregnant again."

Mrs. Jackson drew a sharp breath, and covered her mouth. Her eyes betrayed her own shock at what she'd just revealed.

Emily's heart skipped a beat. "What? What are you talking about? I'm adopted?" she asked horrified.

"Yes, Emily. I didn't plan on telling you like this," she said, trying to recover. "Dad and I meant to tell you years ago, but just never did. It was easier to not talk about it."

"Nooooooo!" screamed Emily. "I can't be. I'm not even yours. All these years! You lied to me! You don't love me. You've never loved me. You lied!"

"Emily, please understand. Your dad and I love you very much," Mrs. Jackson argued, crying harder now.

Marlena felt her eyes become wet with tears. Abruptly, freeing herself from the floor, she ran down the hall way, escaping the pain she heard in her friend's voice.

Grabbing her bicycle, Marlena's slightly chubby legs peddled as fast as they could. Her mind was rampant with thoughts, her brown eyes brimming with tears. Emily's adopted and the Jackson's lied to her all these years. How could they do that? Marlena swallowed the huge lump in her throat that threatened to choke her. If I were adopted, I'd be so mad, especially if they didn't tell me.

I wonder who her parents really are? She has all that stuff the Jackson's bought her, but she doesn't have a real mom and dad. Still, she does have all that stuff I'd like to have, Marlena thought, calming down some.

She rolled into Muddy Creek Park and put the jack stand down. No other children were here today. She walked over to the large swing set and sat down, allowing the gentle swinging motion to continue to calm her, as the air dried her sweaty skin.

Her face felt tight where the tears had traced and her legs ached. Her heart wasn't beating so fast now as she tried to look at her friends' dilemma from a different perspective. Her own.

Well, she still has lots of money, she rationalized, so she can't be mad at her parents for that. That's more than I have. She can still join the Starlighters. They still want her. Hmmmm. Kind of like the Jackson's must have wanted her when they adopted her. Someone has always wanted her, she thought, as a twinge of guilt struck her. But she could still help me get into the club. But what do I say to her now?

"What d-do I say to her now?" she asked herself, audibly, with renewed anger. "She e-even said she wouldn't n-need me if she had a s-sister," she continued, aloud although the only ears to hear were her own. "Where d-does that leave me? Alone! Absolutely a-alone. I wonder if Emily f-feels that way t-too, now? Alone and worse, b-because it's her parents."

Reflecting silently, she thought, at least I do have a sister. She is a pain most of the time, but at least I've got one.

Abruptly Marlena stopped the swing. "Wait a minute," she spoke aloud again, suddenly filled with panic, her mind racing. How many times has Cheryl told me I'm different than the rest of the family and not just about Down Syndrome? I've got dark brown hair and brown eyes. Mom and Dad both have blond hair and blue eyes. Cheryl has light brown hair and green eyes. Even Rachel and Philip have light hair. I'm the only one. I'm short and pudgy. I am totally different. Could they have adopted me? They wouldn't have, would they? What an awful thought! Marlena shivered.

"I'm going down the slide first," she heard a child say, noting for the first time, other children had come to the park.

"I'm second," said another.

Marlena watched the children play. Wonder who their parents are? Are they adopted, too? Or do they have 'real' parents?

Wearily Marlena walked over to her bike. Defeat filled her heart. None of her problems were solved and now she had new ones. Adoption. Emily was adopted for certain and for the first time she questioned her own parentage. "Who am I?" she spoke aloud.

"What?" asked a child near her.

"Oh. N-Never m-mind," Marlena returned. "Just t-talking to m-myself."

The child giggled and ran toward the swing set.

Mounting her bike, Marlena set for home. Relief and quiet fear argued with each other as Marlena neared her home. "I've g-got to know," she said. "I'll j-just h-have to ask!"

"Cheryl, c-can I ask y-you something?" questioned Marlena as soon as she saw her sister.

"Sure, shoot."

"You know h-how you a-always t-tease me about b-being d-different from everyone else in the f-family?"

"Well, you are!" quipped Cheryl.

"J-Just l-listen!"

"Sorry!" Cheryl said tartly.

"Am I a-adopted?"

Cheryl laughed. "Why? Do you want to be?"

"N-No!" retorted Marlena, angrily.

"What's going on?" she asked.

"I j-just n-need to know!"

"I've always thought so," she teased, laughing lightly.

"I'm s-serious," implored Marlena.

"Okay, okay. No, you aren't adopted. I was just messing with you."

"How d-do you know I w-wasn't adopted?" Marlena pressed.

"Because I remember Mom carrying you. Dad took me to the hospital to see you after you were born.

"Will you please tell me what this is all about?" Cheryl indulged, realizing Marlena was clearly upset.

"I c-can't," Marlena responded, fighting the tears filling her eyes.

"Marlena," Cheryl said, pulling her sister into her arms. "What is wrong?"

"I c-can't t-tell you," she repeated, holding tightly to Cheryl. "B-But it's awful. J-Just awful!"

Chapter 7

The Promise

"Do you really think this is a good idea?" asked Carolyn, twirling her hair around her finger nervously.

"Sure, why not?" insisted Judy. "In fact, it's perfect.

"Gail and I have it figured out. Marlena will come and we'll make her promise she can never talk to Emily again, since Emily doesn't want to join. We'll even tell her she can join, as long as, she promises. And of course, as long as, she does the other requirements," she continued, causing the girls to giggle.

"You know," added Judy maliciously, "there is no way she can never speak to Emily again. She won't even be able to explain to her why she can't talk to her. She'll eventually break her promise, assuming of course, she does promise. And she will! She will!"

"Oh look, here she comes," remarked Gail, her eyes twinkling.

"Hi g-guys," grinned Marlena as cheerfully as she could.

"Hi!" the girls responded in near unison.

"Here's my camera I told you, you could use," offered Carolyn, extending the device toward her.

"Th-Thanks!" beamed Marlena. "It m-means a lot that you'd l-loan it t-to me. I'll be careful with it."

"No problem," answered Carolyn, genuinely. "Here let me show you how it works. Here's the zoom….."

"Okay, okay. Let's walk around and see if we get lucky," interrupted Judy, walking away, annoyed.

"Wow, is that ever pretty," commented Gail, more as a statement than a question.

"W-What?" asked Marlena, looking in the direction Gail had been.

"That huge azalea bush. That's the biggest one I've ever seen. Those are my mom's favorite kind of plant," she continued, while snapping some pictures.

"You okay?" Carolyn probed.

"S-Sure. I'm f-fine," Marlena lied. "Why?"

"You seem distracted. You haven't even taken any pictures."

"Oh d-don't w-worry. I just h-haven't seen anything th-that c-catches my eye yet."

"Okay," Carolyn conceded, shrugging her shoulders.

"So how are your initiation requirements coming along?"

"Oh, th-they are. I'm w-working on it. I still h-have three d-days."

"Oh, we know," interjected Gail. "We thought maybe we'd make it a little easier for you."

"H-How?" doubted Marlena, but suddenly alert.

"Well, if Emily doesn't want to join, fine. You can join our club, as long as, you do all your requirements with the exception of the one about Emily having to join." Gail paused, waiting for the reaction to the information to sink in.

Marlena could barely contain her excitement. "Oh m-my g-gosh," she gushed, her eyes open wide. "Y-You m-mean it? I c-can j-join?"

"Well, there is one little thing. Like I said, you still have to fulfill the other requirements."

"Y-Yeah," breathed Marlena, suddenly feeling shrouded in darkness and cold, fearful of what would come next.

"You are never to speak to Emily again. Not ever for any reason."

"Never?" whispered Marlena, shocked speechless.

"Absolutely never!" emphasized Gail.

"W-Wow! H-How am I supposed t-to d-do that? She's b-been my best f-friend since K-Kindergarten."

"I can't help that. If she doesn't want to be part of our group, then she won't. And if you're going to be part of our group, you'll do like the group decides. Which includes," Gail added harshly, "No Emily!"

"Okay, y-you d-don't have to be m-mean about it. I c-can do that," she groaned.

"You'll never speak to her again; in any form?" Judy demanded.

"N-Never," Marlena agreed sadly. "B-Besides, d-didn't you n-notice t-today? We n-never even t-talked to each other once. She a-avoided m-me and I avoided h-her."

I don't know what I'd say to her even if I could, she continued quietly in her thoughts. Maybe this is meant to be after all. No matter how she tried, however, the heaviness and grief that lodged in her heart, refused to budge.

"Good! It's settled. We still have time to walk around and get a few more pictures."

"Oh m-my g-gosh! T-Time! What t-time is it?" gushed Marlena, panicky.

"3:45. Why?" inquired Carolyn.

"I h-have an ap-pointment with J-Judge S-Simms at 4."

"What? Are you kidding?" asked Gail incredulously.

"W-Well, yeah. It was p-part of the initiation r-requirement. R-Remember?" she added more sarcastically than she intended.

"Well, sure I remember. I just didn't think."

Marlena cut her off. "N-No, you d-didn't think I c-could do it. D-Did you?" she challenged.

"Sure I did," Gail replied, recovering. "It just didn't occur to me you'd make an appointment."

"How else w-would I have g-gotten his s-stupid l-lock of h-hair? S-Sneak into his h-house while he was a-asleep?"

"I guess I didn't think about how you'd do it."

"N-No k-kidding. I've g-got to go. Th-Thanks again for the u-use of your c-camera, C-Carolyn. I'll d-drop the few pictures I t-took off at the one hour photo shop on my way to see Judge S-Simms. I'll b-bring the p-pictures to school t-tomorrow."

Marlena entered the court house. The clock on the wall said 3:58. "I m-made it," she said aloud. Her voice echoed in the large, high ceilinged room. She read the signs: Licenses; Permits; Information. Concluding 'Information' was her best option, she walked timidly toward the lady behind the counter. "Hello?"

"Hello," she responded, smiling. "Can I help you."

"I h-have an ap-pointment with J-Judge S-Simms."

"You do? Are you sure? He doesn't usually make appointments with young people your age."

"Yes, M-Ma'am. I c-called and m-made an ap-appointment for 4:00 o'clock."

"Let me see," she said, thumbing through a notebook. "What's your name?"

"M-Marlena R-Richardson."

"Oh yes. Here you are. Hold on just one moment please, while I phone his office."

"Betsy, a Marlena Richardson is here to see the Judge. Okay. I'll tell her. Thanks," Marlena heard.

"Judge Simms went out about an hour ago and hasn't yet returned. He should be back any time if you'd care to wait."

"Th-thank you," Marlena squeaked. "M-May I use the phone, p-please?"

"There's a pay phone right down the hall, Dear."

"Th-Thank you," Marlena said again, jamming her hands into her pockets hoping to find change there.

Hurriedly, Marlena went to the telephone, ruing the fact she didn't have her own cell phone. She counted the change in her hands. $.50. Just enough, she thought, punching in the numbers to her house.

"Cheryl, this is M-Marlena," she started without preamble. "T-Tell M-Mom I'll be home s-soon. I stayed after for p-pictures for the n-newspaper contest and I'm r-running b-behind."

"Well, what time do you think you'll be home? It is supposed to storm tonight."

"I d-don't know. S-Soon!" she spat.

"Sorry," countered Cheryl, sounding wounded.

"N-No. I am. I'll b-be there s-soon. Th-That's the b-best I can g-give you."

"Okay. Oh, and by the way, Adam Blake called. You two a thing now?" she teased.

"N-No! Oh, n-never m-mind," Marlena replied roughly. "J-Just n-never mind. I've g-got to go. B-Be home soon."

"Bye," answered Cheryl, feeling guilty for taunting her sister. Wish I knew what was wrong with her, she thought.

Marlena jammed her hand in her pockets once again, this time feeling the plastic bag and hoping to find some confidence there. "Excuse m-me, M-Ma'am. Where sh-should I wait f-for J-Judge S-Simms?"

"Oh, I'm sorry, Sweetie. Go up on the second floor, turn right. You'll see his secretary. Wait there."

"Th-Thank you." Marlena nearly crept up the stairs in fright. Regardless of her efforts to stay quiet, it seemed every sound echoed in the large opened building. Her heart pounded while her mind was racing with questions. How am I ever going to ask Judge Simms for a lock of his hair? Judge I need a lock of your hair. She laughed at the idea. Will you let me cut a lock of your hair Judge Simms? I need it for a school project. She scowled at the thought. Trying again, she thought, Judge this is a matter of life or death. I desperately need a lock of your hair. Marlena shivered. *What in the world have I gotten myself into?* she wondered.

"I'm h-here to see J-Judge S-Simms," Marlena spoke softly to the secretary.

"Really? You have an appointment?"

"Yes, M-Ma-am. At f-four o-clock."

"Marlena Richardson?"

"Yes, M-Ma-am."

"I didn't expect a child. Have a seat, Dear. He's just returned. He'll see you in a moment."

"B-But? Yes, M-Ma-am." Marlena swallowed her question. *How did he get past me and I not see him? I was right in the hall!*

"Miss Richardson, Judge Simms will see you now."

"Th-Thank you," she offered, standing.

Marlena entered the large, ornate office. Books lined the wall. Judge Simms sat behind an oversized desk, filled with papers and stacks of neatly organized folders. She stopped abruptly. "What?"

"Something wrong, young lady?" asked Judge Simms, his forehead furrowed in lines. "You're as white as a ghost. You did want to see me, didn't you?"

"Y-Yes S-Sir. But?" Marlena felt sick. Her knees were about to give out from under her. She reached for the back of the chair to steady herself.

"What is the matter, Miss Richardson? Can I get you something?" he asked now standing, clearly concerned.

"Y-Your h-hair!"

"My hair?"

"You have a c-crew c-cut!" she nearly screamed.

"Yes I do, Miss Richardson. I just came from the barber. I always get a crew cut this time of year. Is there something wrong with that?"

"W-Wrong? You j-just ruined m-my l-life. H-How c-could you do that?"

"I don't understand. What does my crew cut have to do with ruining your life?"

"Everything," she replied, nearly in tears. "E-Everything."

Judge Simms continued toward her. "Now see here, young lady."

"I-I've g-got to go," she said abruptly. "I've g-got to go." Turning she bolted from the room, leaving Judge Simms standing in total confusion.

"Miss Mace. What was that all about?"

"I don't have a clue," the secretary stated. "She just ran through here and headed for the stairs."

Marlena stopped so suddenly from an idea that popped in her head, she nearly fell. Turning, she retraced her steps up the stairs coming face to face once more with Judge Simms.

Breathless and without preamble, she asked. "W-What b-barber did you g-go to?"

"Excuse me?"

"B-Barber. What b-barber just cut your hair? I h-have to know!" she insisted.

"Harold's Hair House on Ladner Road. Why?"

"J-Judge S-Simms, you're w-wonderful. Y-You just s-saved my l-life," she gushed, charging toward him. Flinging her arms around his waist, she gave him a quick squeeze. "Th-Thank you," she said again, fleeing from the room, leaving both the startled Judge and surprised secretary wondering what just happened.

Exhilarated, with a spring in her step, Marlena made her way, as quick as she could, to Harold's Hair House. Gingerly, Marlena opened the door. Four sets of eyes turned to look at her; two older gentlemen waiting for their turn in the chair, a middle-aged man currently getting a haircut and the barber.

"Can I help you, Miss?" asked the barber.

"D-Did you just c-cut Judge S-Simms h-hair?"

"Excuse me?"

"D-Did y-you just cut Judge S-Simms h-hair?" she repeated, exasperated.

"Yes, I did. Why?"

"I n-need his h-hair."

"Excuse me?" said the bewildered barber, yet again.

Talking between clenched teeth, Marlena spoke quietly, yet loud enough to be heard. "I n-need his h-hair, a l-lock of it f-for a school p-project. Where is it?"

"In the trash can over there," he motioned.

Malena looked in the trash can. "Is h-his hair on t-top?" she asked, noting the several different shades of brown there.

"Yeah, it would be. I cut his last," he shrugged.

"D-Do you h-have a t-tissue?"

"Excuse me?"

Fighting the urge to scream at the man, she repeated slowly. "D-Do you h-have a t-tissue? I d-don't want to p-pick it up with m-my h-hands."

"Oh. Yes. On the counter to your right."

Carefully Marlena picked up the hair in the tissue. Reaching in her pocket she took out the plastic bag. "Oh!" she said becoming more frustrated.

"W-Would you o-open this f-for me?" she asked.

"I'll do it, Missy," said one of the older gentlemen in the chair waiting his turn. "Harold is kind of busy there, cutting Frank's hair. A school project, huh? They didn't have projects like this when I was in school."

"N-No Sir," she said, without offering any further information.

"Thank you, S-Sir," was all she could manage, while trying to reply kindly, her nerves taunt. Placing the tissue and hair in the bag, she zipped it and breathed a sigh of relief.

"Th-Thank you, th-thank you," she repeated, making a quick exit before any more questions or comments could be made.

"I did it! I really did it!" she grinned, congratulating herself audibly, to no one in particular. Her mind raced. *I really got some of Judge Simms hair. And they didn't think I could! Who am I kidding? I wasn't sure I could do it,* she thought ruefully, reaching into her pocket, reassuring herself the prized possession remained. *I really get to be a Starlighter. I really, really do!*

I better hurry, Marlena admonished herself. *It looks like it could pour.* Thunder rolled in the distance. As the clouds moved overhead, a cloud moved into Marlena's heart. *I just wish there wasn't this mess with Emily. How am I ever going be able to keep my promise? What's Mom going to say when she finds out?*

All this time Em's been my best friend. Who am I going to have sleep over? Marlena shivered. The Starlighters! She answered steeling herself against the onslaught of quiet accusations in her mind. They'll be my best friends. It has to be this way. I deserve to be a Starlighter. Besides, it's Emily's fault she isn't one. Not mine. It's all her, she reasoned.

Chapter Eight

The Picture

Breathless, Marlena opened the door to Revaton Middle. Slipping inside, she darted to the nearest open classroom door. She waited, fearing discovery. Behind the door, she could hear familiar voices.

"Where did Marlena go, Terri?" asked Emily. "I know I saw her come in here. I can't believe she didn't hear me call her. I wanted to show her the pictures we took on the camping trip."

"Sorry, I didn't see her. Can I see the pictures, though?"

"Sure."

"They're good. I like this one. That fawn looks just like Bambi."

"I like it, too. I really wanted Marlena's opinion though."

"Are you and she still partners?" Terri asked cautiously.

"I don't know. I guess not. She wants to be a Starlighter now."

"That amazes me. Who would have thought that Marlena, of all people, would've wanted to be part of them?"

"Not me," Emily responded, dejectedly.

"You okay?"

"Sure, why?"

"Well, I know this "Marlena, Starlighter" thing is weird, and must make you feel awful. But yesterday you looked sick and you don't look like you feel much better today."

"Don't worry about it. Just some stuff with my folks, and like you said, this Marlena thing. I'll be all right," she emphasized, trying to convince herself, as well as, her friend.

"Well, okay," said Terri, not sure she believed her. "Oh, there's the bell. I've got to hurry, or I'm going to be late. See ya at lunch."

"What are you doing in my class, young lady?" asked Mrs. Burd, startling Marlena.

"Uh, uh…. N-Nothing. H-Honest," she mumbled, inching her way into the hall. "I've got to hurry or I'm going to be late," she added, moving down the hall as quickly as she could without running.

This is awful! How am I supposed to do this? "I don't know, I just don't know!" she said aloud.

"Excuse me?" said Mr. Bakworth, as she entered her Geography class.

Blushing, Marlena said, "N-Nothing," while taking her seat just two spots in front of Emily, avoiding her eyes. As she sat down, the bell rang for the second time. She'd just made it!

That was close, she thought. First escaping Emily before school; thank goodness Terri didn't see me. Then being caught by Mrs. Burd and then almost being late for class. And next period, Emily is in there again. I've got to be more careful, and time this better! This is going to be tougher than I thought. Thank goodness we only have two classes together. Oh yuck! And Health. But at least that's not until tomorrow!

"Marlena, are you with us?"

"P-Pardon m-me?"

"Pay attention. We're waiting on you to pass your homework forward."

"S-Sorry," she said, grimacing and red-faced.

"Hmm," said Mr. Bakworth. "Sorry indeed. Just stay with us. Okay?"

"Y-Yes sir," Marlena said meekly.

Marlena walked the long way to Math class. Avoiding Emily was not only emotionally draining, but physically too. It meant walking twice as far and twice as fast to get to the same place. Still, this is the only way, she consoled herself. I aim to be somebody! I am going to be a Starlighter!

Just before the second bell ran, Marlena, out of breath, entered Mr. Baylor's Math class. It was the first time since school started she was glad her seat wasn't near Emily's but across the room toward the back. She'd always hated it there, but not today.

As soon as the bell rang for the end of class, Marlena sprang from her seat and darted out the door. "Marlena wait," she heard Emily call. "I need to talk to you!"

Marlena's pace quickened, fighting the urge to turn around.

Marlena!" called Terri. "Where are you going in such a hurry? Don't you have English with Mrs. O next?"

"Y-Yeah," she answered gruffly.

"This isn't the way," Terri countered, bewildered.

"I know. I j-just wanted t-to go the l-long w-way."

"The long way?"

"Y-Yeah, you know, the l-long way as o-opposed to the sh-short way. I'll g-get there. It j-just t-takes l-longer."

"What is wrong with you?" she laughed. "You're being weird. And you'd better hurry up. The bell's about to ring!" she added.

"I know. B-Bye," Marlena said, sprinting down another hall, hoping no teachers were on the lookout.

"Marlena Richardson. Slow down!" commanded Mrs. O, as Marlena nearly crashed into her, in the doorway.

"S-Sorry," she apologized, hurrying to her seat.

"Class…" began Mrs. O.

Marlena hardly heard her. Her mind spun in a thousand different directions while her heart wrestled with her conscience. Finally, the bell signaled the end of class.

This time Marlena rose slowly, in no particular rush to leave the room. Walking to her locker, she didn't see or hear anyone; still wrapped in the world warring in her mind. I've got to get in control of this, she reprimanded herself. I'm too close now to let silly friendships alter my goal. This is absolutely the right thing to do.

Retrieving her lunch from her locker, she headed toward the cafeteria with new, set determination. I will be; *I am* a Starlighter, she corrected herself.

Choosing to come into the cafeteria through the side doors to eliminate the need to walk toward her old lunch table, she headed straight for the Starlighters.

"H-Hi g-guys!" she said with as much enthusiasm, as she could muster. Placing her lunch on the table she painted on her best smile and added matter-of-factly, "I'm g-going to go b-buy ice c-cream. I'll b-be right b-back."

Taking an empty chair from another table upon her return, Marlena wedged herself between Carolyn and Judy.

"The pictures we took from the infamous camping trip and our more successful walk at the Muddy Creek Park are back," Gail informed anyone who was listening.

Marlena cringed at the comment of the 'infamous camping trip.' What a disaster that had been. That was when things really started going badly between Em and me, she thought sadly.

Feeling the nudge of Judy's elbow in her side, Marlena jumped. "Are you with us?" she asked.

"W-What?"

"Here!" said Gail annoyed, handing her the pictures. "Pass these to Judy. And you can look at them too, if you want."

"Oh, th-thanks," she said, absently.

"These are from the Park. They're the best."

"Not bad," agreed Judy. "Now we have to decide which one to use."

"Oh, don't worry. We will," Carolyn commented, quietly.

"I can't wait until Friday night," Judy said, changing the subject. "The dance should be so much fun. Just three more nights, including tonight," she added, absently chewing on the ends of her hair. "Hey, who's got dates?"

"Jay hasn't asked yet, but I know he will," Gail stated smugly.

"Ricky already asked me," said Judy, gloating. "He is just the cutest thing."

"Is Adam going to ask you, Carolyn? He is sort of in our little group."

"I don't know. Besides no one says you have to have a date."

"Course you don't," said Judy apologetically. "Just the same, I'll bet he asks you."

"How about you Marlena? You have a date?"

"N-No. N-Not yet," she said, shyly, blushing.

"Maybe there's someone out there who'll ask you," Judy said, taunting her.

"Yeah, m-maybe," Marlena said, suddenly feeling moisture rise on her forehead and around her neckline.

"Well, has anyone decided what they're wearing?" asked Gail, changing the subject.

"If the dance is the Hawaiian theme, then all we have to wear is grass skirts," laughed Judy.

"I'm serious," replied Gail, trying to collect herself from hysteria. "What are you going to wear? We don't have much time left."

"You know, I read somewhere that originally hula dancers were topless," commented Carolyn. "Can you imagine?"

"N-No! I sure c-can't," answered Marlena. "H-How embarrassing."

"My mom brought back some hula skits when she went to Hawaii three years ago," offered Patti Cooper, who had joined the girls just moments before.

"How many?" asked Gail excitedly. "Is there enough for all of us?"

"I know she brought back three, maybe four because there was one for me, my sister, her and I think she said," unsure of herself as she counted, "that she brought one back for my cousin, Megan."

"But four isn't enough," said Marlena alarmed.

"Well, you'll have to wear a muu muu or something," quipped Judy gleefully. "There's one for each of the Starlighters."

"B-But I'm a S-Starlighter," maintained Marlena defensively. "W-Well I'm g-going to b-be one."

"Well, maybe. But you're not one yet."

"I think I can get the leis we need," offered Carolyn. "They're the silk, flowered ones, not real, of course. My Aunt Sheila brought quite a few back when she and Uncle Mac went over some years ago. I'm sure she'll let us borrow those."

"What do you do for a top, Patti?" questioned Gail. "You said you have the skirts."

"Wear a swimsuit," she answered confidently. "Mom brought back lots of pictures and she said that's what they wear under them."

"Good! It's settled, then," declared Judy. "Except for you, Marlena. I guess you're on your own."

"Th-Thanks," she huffed, disgustedly.

"Sorrr-rry!" retorted Judy, sarcastically.

"Oh, I almost forgot!" cried Gail. "I have one more picture from the camping trip I have just got to show you. This is the best one, too! Look!" she said, holding it high so everyone could see.

Marlena gasped. Those around her exploded with laughter. "That's E-Emily when she f-fell," she exclaimed, completely mortified.

"No kidding!" crowed Gail, as renewed laughter swept the group again. "I think this is the one we should use for the contest."

"Th-That's awful!" fumed Marlena. "H-How c-can you s-say that?"

"Easy!" goaded Gail, trying to contain her laughter. "This is the picture we should use for the contest!"

"Y-You know, s-sometimes I think E-Emily was r-right. You g-guys are awful. She's a n-nice p-person and j-just b-because she won't join your c-club you want to em-embarrass her."

"Marlena, calm down," said Carolyn. "We're just teasing. We're not using that one. It'll be one of the pictures from Muddy Creek Park. We're just messing with you."

"Thank goodness for that!" said Emily, startling the group.

"Emily," consoled Carolyn. "We were really kidding. Honest."

Pushing her chair back roughly, Marlena stood and picked up her books. Without saying a word, she ran out of the cafeteria. As she turned the corner into the hall, she ran square into Adam Blake. Books and papers went everywhere.

"Marlena! I'm sorry. I didn't see you coming. Here let me help you pick up this mess."

Turning Marlena saw the students behind her and heard snickering. Trying to ignore the growing crowd, she mumbled, "It's f-fine. It's all m-my f-fault. I wasn't watching w-where I was g-going."

"Are you all right?" he asked, when they finished retrieving all the school supplies.

"I'm f-fine. Honest."

"I wanted to see you," he said, shyly. "Would you be my date for the dance on Friday night?"

"Y-You want me to b-be your d-date?" she asked incredulously.

"Well, yeah, if you'd like to be."

"F-Fine! Just f-fine!" she said, running once again, biting back tears.

Chapter Nine

The Decision

"I c-can't b-believe it's Thursday already," said Marlena, as she reached Carolyn's locker in the hall.

"I know. Me either!" agreed Carolyn, turning to face the others. "And tomorrow night's the dance."

"You did turn the picture in, right?" verified Judy, turning to face Gail.

"Yeah. I went to see Mrs. Brennen on my way in this morning. She wasn't there, so I gave it to Miss Schmidt. I'm glad too, because I sure don't like Mrs. Brennen much."

"W-Why? What's w-wrong with h-her?" questioned Marlena.

"She makes Home Ec boring," replied Gail.

"Oh I d-don't think s-so," Marlena protested cheerfully. "I enjoy h-her c-class."

"You would," Gail answered sarcastically.

"W-What d-does that m-mean?"

"You like all weird people."

"I d-do n-not!"

"That's your opinion."

110

"Never mind, you two," countered Carolyn. "As long as Mrs. Brennen gets the picture, we're set."

"Which one d-did we d-decide on anyway?" inquired Marlena.

"Oh, it doesn't matter to you. You have your own pictures, don't you? Haven't you gotten yours back yet? You said you were going to bring them in. Did I miss it?" asked Gail.

"Well, y-yeah, I d-did have p-pictures," said Marlena, answering the first question first. "A-And yes, I d-did g-get them b-back. B-But the focus was off and the p-pictures really d-didn't t-turn out that g-good.

"B-But I d-don't g-get it. D-Don't I get included with the p-picture t-turned in from the Starlighters? We d-did g-go to Muddy C-Creek P-Park together. R-Remember? You in-invited m-me!"

"Sure I remember inviting you to come with us. But," Gail paused deliberately. "You aren't a Starlighter yet. Remember?"

"H-How c-could I f-forget?" groused Marlena.

"Don't worry. I'm sure there will be a picture there in your name, even if yours didn't turn out," giggled Judy.

"W-What are you t-talking about?"

"Oh nothing," she smirked. "You joining us for lunch tomorrow?"

"Y-Yeah. Th-Thanks," she replied, uneasily.

"Okay, got to get home. Mom is expecting me. We'll see you then," Gail interjected smugly.

A knot formed at the bottom of Marlena's stomach. What now? She wondered.

Friday morning went by slowly. Emily no longer pursued Marlena. It was as though they no longer knew each other. Marlena hurt inside, torn between her loss of Emily as a friend and her desire to join the Starlighters. Even though the sun shone brightly through the windows of the rooms, birds sang overhead, and her favorite smell of freshly cut grass wafted through the windows, Marlena remained gloomy and sad.

Smells of food, overpowering the scent of cut grass, greeted Marlena long before she entered the lunch room. "H-Hi e-everyone," she said, in her cheeriest voice. "S-Sorry I'm l-late. Th-There was a fight near my l-locker and I h-had to t-take the l-long way around to get here."

"No problem," assured Judy.

"I'll b-be right b-back," said Marlena, rushing to put her books down. "I've g-got to h-hurry and get l-lunch before they c-close the d-doors.

"That was c-close," she said when she returned. "I was the n-next to the l-last p-person in l-line."

Marlena ate her lunch in silence while the girls talked all around her. Nearing the completion of her meal, she finally found the courage to ask. "Is th-there s-something wrong w-with me? You g-guys s-seemed eager enough to h-have me join you for l-lunch y-yesterday afternoon-noon, b-but no one has s-said a s-single word to me s-since I s-sat d-down. Why?" she demanded.

"Well, now that you ask," articulated Gail, "I guess it's up to me, since I am President of the Starlighters to explain."

Marlena felt a cold chill sweep over her body. "W-What's g-goin on?" she asked, suddenly afraid of the answer.

"Well, we've decided you can't join our club after all."

Marlena's heart sank. "W-Why?" she asked, stunned. "B-Besides I have until t-tonight."

"No, it's right now. Remember we said you have until the night of the dance. Well, it's afternoon and that's close enough, so your time has run out."

"B-But I d-did everything you asked," she pleaded. "I j-joined f-four c-clubs, gave f-flowers to Adam B-Blake."

The girls erupted in laughter and Marlena reddened.

"And I g-got Judge S-Simms hair," she stated, matter-of-factly. "And you g-guys said you didn't want E-Emily in the g-group anymore, as long as, I p-promised to n-never to t-talk to her and I haven't," she concluded, swallowing tears.

"That's true, you did do most of those things," agreed Judy, trying to contain her mirth. "And you've been a real good sport, too. But tell me how you possibly got Judge Simms hair. We haven't seen that one yet."

"W-Well, he g-got it c-cut just before I went to see h-him, so I went to the b-barber and got it. L-Look," she said opening her book bag. "It's right here."

"You actually got that from the barber shop?" asked Carolyn, clearly perplexed.

"Y-Yes I d-did," whispered Marlena, barley keeping her anger below the surface.

"You can't be sure or prove that it's his hair. It could be anybody's!" insisted Gail.

"Besides, even though you haven't spoken to Emily since you promised, you did defend her the other day when you saw the picture of her in the mud. You remember; we suggested using it for the contest?"

"W-What is wrong with th-that?" Marlena demanded.

"Marlena," Gail began exasperated, "she is still your friend, even if you don't talk to her. And who knows," she goaded, "that picture just might win a prize."

"Wh-What?" shot Marlena, now fully angry. "Wh-What p-picture? Y-You said."

"We didn't," Judy cut off. "Not in our name anyway," she added under her breath.

Laughter again erupted around her. "Y-You g-guys are awful," she hissed. "I'm g-glad I c-can't join your s-stupid g-group. I wouldn't now even if you wanted me. You're m-mean and h-hateful. I was wrong to ever want to be a S-Starlighter!"

Picking up her things, Marlena turned to leave. Startled, she stopped abruptly. She was face to face with Emily. She felt water building around her eyes. Unable to fight the natural forces, she felt the hot tears slip down her cheeks. For a moment, their eyes locked. Without a word, Marlena fled the room.

"You guys are so cruel," said Emily in a low seething voice. "Marlena is the nicest person I know and you guys hurt her for the pure pleasure of it. She is kind, honest, sincere and really thought being a Starlighter would be special.

"Yes, she has Down Syndrome and that makes her different. Maybe that's why you didn't want her. But she's beautiful! I have Dyslexia. I suppose if you'd known that, you wouldn't have wanted me either. You guys aren't special. You're just plain mean."

With her words spoken, Emily walked away.

For a moment, no one spoke. "We really are mean," agreed Carolyn, regretfully. "I wish we hadn't done that."

"Oh, come on!" cajoled Gail. "It was all in fun. She'll get over it."

"I hope you're right. Honestly, I'm not sure I will," sighed Carolyn. "You know everyone around here just heard what happened. It's going to be all over school."

"Who cares?" asked Judy glibly. "Let it. We're still the Starlighters. We're still the best!"

"I'm not so sure anymore," lamented Carolyn.

Chapter Ten

The Dance

"Mom, I don't want to go," whined Emily.

"You're going," insisted Mrs. Jackson. "You don't have to talk to Marlena if you don't want to," she said, hugging her daughter. "I know this is hard for you, but I'm sure it will all work out eventually. Besides, your dad and I have to go. I promised Mrs. Brennen we would be chaperones."

"But, Mom."

"No buts. You've got a cute Hawaiian outfit. I know you've turned in a picture for the photo contest and who knows, maybe you'll win."

"Who cares about that dumb contest. I just did it because Marlena wanted to."

"I know. But now that you did, you need to see it through. Scoot now. Go get dressed. I'll help you if you need it."

"Mom…"

"Go!"

Reluctantly, Emily went to her room. She traced the bright purple leaves and flower pattern that splashed against the sea blue of her dress. "A muu muu," she said aloud. "What a funny name for a dress."

"She touched the velvet softness of the purple orchid petals that matched her dress. "Paradise," she whispered with a heavy heart. "It sure won't feel much like paradise tonight."

___ ___ ___

"Hurry up, Marlena. You'll make us late," scolded Cheryl.

"I know," sniffled Marlena. "I f-feel like such an id-idiot. I don't know if I sh-should g-go anyway. I am so h-humiliated. You can s-say I t-told you so, y-you know."

"I know I can, but I won't. Chalk it up to experience. The point is you can't choose your friends because of how popular or fashionable you think they are. Emily's been your best friend for forever. You need to make up."

"I'm t-too embarrassed. B-Besides she p-probably thinks I d-deserved it. She'd be r-right. I was a j-jerk.

"A-And what a-about A-Adam?" Marlena continued.

"What about him?" her sister challenged.

"H-He asked m-me to the d-dance. He p-probably d-did it b-because he thought I was g-going to be a S-Starlighter."

"If that's true then you wouldn't want to be at the dance with him anyway. If he asked you to be with him at the dance because he likes you, then you'd better hurry and get ready. We're going to be late if you don't," she admonished her.

"B-But I d-don't know!" Marlena shouted.

"Well, you'll never find out just sitting there! Hurry up!" Cheryl pointed out, ignoring the agitation her sister clearly felt.

— — —

"Is this cool or what?" bubbled Judy. "Never have I seen anything so beautiful."

"Wow!" breathed Carolyn. "How did they do this?"

The gym was transformed into paradise. In the far-right corner standing majestically, was a model of Diamond Head, the extinct volcano from the island of Oahu.

Sand was spread the length of the room with a water mural on the back wall depicting the ocean. The sound of the ocean reaching the shore, intermingled with the Hawaiian music floating softy from the likeness created from the famed Polynesian Cultural Center at the far-left side of the room. The south pacific Villages of Tahiti, Samoa, Fiji, Hawaii, New Zealand, Tong and the Marquesas featured shows and demonstrations representative of every island.

Foods of the islands were available at each of the villages including poi, pineapple, baked ulu (breadfruit), pip kuala (beef jerky), papaya, pig and other Hawaiian juices and fruits.

To the right front, the area was transformed to represent the Waimea Falls Park. Hawaiian flora swayed in the gentle breeze, created by fans high above, while murals of the Falls covered that area of the walls. Remains of an early Hawaiian community completed the picture.

The center of the floor which would later be used for dance, was currently filled with students in Hawaiian attire.

"This is incredible," said Gail. "Absolutely incredible."

"Oh look, there's Adam," remarked Carolyn.

"Did he ever ask you to the dance?" questioned Gail.

"No. I heard he asked someone else, but I'm not sure who."

"Well, here's my date," grinned Gail. "Jay just walked in and it looks like Ricky's with him."

"You're right," confirmed Judy. "I'm glad they said they'd meet us here, instead of our parents bringing us separately. This way we could all come together!" With skirts swaying, the girls made their way toward the boys.

Marlena came through the open doors as the Starlighters were weaving their way through the crowd. She noted Adam to her right, near Waimea Falls Park. He looked handsome in his striking white shorts against his golden tan. He wore a leaf headpiece with beads around his neck and ankles. He hadn't noticed her yet, and she was grateful.

Moving away, she also noted the Starlighters, who were so intent on their own purposes, hadn't seen her. "Aren't we dressed just perfectly?" she heard Gail ask as they reached Jay and Ricky.

Marlena wandered about the Paradise. She, too was awed by how beautiful it was. "S-Someday," she said aloud without realizing she'd used her voice.

"Me, too."

Turning she saw Adam. "W-What?"

"Someday, me, too."

"S-Someday, you t-too, what?"

"Someday, I'm really going to Hawaii."

"H-How did you know th-that's what I was th-thinking?"

"I just did and you're right. It's beautiful and so are you."

Marlena blushed, unable to speak.

"Let's dance," Adam said, reaching for her hand. "I saw a sign that said to take our shoes off and go barefoot in the sand while dancing," he explained, as Marlena noted him removing his.

"I'm n-not a S-Starlighter," she stated, simply, with only a hint of regret.

"I didn't ask if you were," he chuckled, his eyes twinkling.

"B-But I th-thought."

"You thought I asked you to be my date because you were going to be a Starlighter?"

"W-Well yeah. D-Didn't you?"

"No."

"B-But you're p-part of their g-group. Aren't you just s-supposed to ask g-girls f-from the Starlighters to d-dance and s-stuff like that?"

"No, I am not part of their group. They're all right, I guess. But I like you."

"E-Even though I-I'm," she faltered, "d-different?"

"Yup! Just like you are! So, are you going to dance with me or not?"

"Well, okay," Marlena whispered, kicking her shoes off; not sure she'd heard correctly, since her heart was pounding so loudly.

"Can I get you something to drink?" asked Adam, when the dance was finished.

"Th-Thanks. I'd l-like that," she said, more relaxed now.

Taking her hand, they walked toward the villages. "You know," Adam began cautiously, "You need to find Emily and set things right between you."

"I c-can't. I was awful t-to her. I c-can't f-face her. B-Besides, you d-don't know everything. In f-fact, h-how do y-you know anything about Em-Emily and m-me?'

"Let's just say, I know enough. And yes, you can face her," he insisted gently. "Did you know she defended you at lunch today when you ran out of the cafeteria?"

"W-What are y-you t-talking about?" she asked, shuddering like she was suddenly cold.

"Emily chewed the Starlighters out good at lunch time and she's right; you're nice, kind, and all those other things she said."

Marlena felt herself blush again. "W-Why are you s-saying all th-this?" she asked warily.

"Because I like you and Emily said those things because she's your friend. Besides," he explained with a smile working at his mouth, "you send nice flowers!"

Marlena tensed. "Th-Thanks!" she lashed out, suddenly angry.

"Marlena, calm down. I was just teasing. Honest. I know why you did that and that took a lot of courage. I know you are strong. Are you going to talk to Emily?"

"I d-don't know," she answered uneasily.

"Well, I do," Adam laughed. "C-mon. Let's dance again!"

Feeling amazingly wonderful, Marlena smiled. "Y-You m-mean it, d-don't you?"

"Yup! I do!" he smiled back, taking her hand. "I sure do!"

"Ladies and Gentlemen," came Mrs. Brennen's voice over the intercom. "Before anymore dances, I have a few announcements to make.

"I'd like to thank the Newspaper Club from Revaton Middle School for the Photo Contest they sponsored and the other supporting clubs for working together for this wonderful Hawaiian themed dance. I'd also like to thank all the local businesses that contributed to the prize money the winners receive."

After the cheering subsided, she continued. "I'd like to announce the winners of the photo contest now, as well. We had some very interesting entries. They were all very good and we appreciate everyone's efforts."

"Honorable mention goes to a group entry, the Starlighters. Second runner up is Nancy Peterman, and first runner up goes to Andy Stokes. Congratulations to all of you. And now, the winner is a combined entry, by Emily Jackson and Marlena Richardson."

"Wh-What?" Marlena gasp. "B-But?"

"Go on up there!" shouted Adam above the noise. "It doesn't matter! Just go!"

Marlena and Emily reached the stage at the same time. Marlena was startled to note her outfit was very similar to Emily's. Some things don't change, she thought happily. We still have the same taste in clothes, even if she can afford the more expensive ones; then immediately regretted the after thought.

"I told her we were partners," Emily whispered quietly.

"B-But what p-picture?"

"I'd like to congratulate you girls on the winning photo," said Mrs. Brennen in the microphone.

"The picture of a doe and her fawn, which will be blown into an eight by ten, will be framed and displayed in the lobby of our school. Because it was a duel entry, we've decided each of the girls will receive the entire $25.00 prize for their efforts. It will be in the Revaton County Newspaper and they have the opportunity to place it in competition in the County Photography Contest next month."

"Thank you very much," said Emily.

"Y-Yes, th-thank you," Marlena echoed. "I sure am s-surprised."

"You deserved it," said Mrs. Brennen, beaming.

The girls turned to leave. "Marlena, may I see you a moment?"

"Sure. Be right back," she told Emily.

"Come by my room on Monday morning. I have a picture on my desk that was turned in to me in your name and I think you should, well, do with it what you'd like. I don't believe it was meant to be in the contest."

Marlena momentarily froze. "W-What p-picture? I d-didn't t-turn one in," she stammered.

"It's of Emily and I didn't think you had. But it was on my desk in a sealed envelope. Just come by and pick it up, okay?"

"Th-Thanks," said Marlena feeling sick. "I w-will."

"You okay?" asked Adam, as she neared the edge of the stage.

"N-No. B-But I will b-be."

"What's wrong?" asked Emily. "What did Mrs. Brennen want?"

"It d-doesn't m-matter now," offered Marlena, beginning to feel better knowing the rift between her and her friend was over. "It j-just d-doesn't m-matter."

"How about I take you both for an ice cream after the dance to celebrate?" Adam asked, squeezing Marlena's hand.

"Thanks," said Emily. "I'd like that."

"Me t-too," Marlena smiled, returning his squeeze. "Me t-too!"